Advance Praise for *Pray*

"PrayerWalk will start a revolution! If you apply the principles of this book, you will not only discover miraculous answers to your prayers, you will also streamline your waistline and benefit emotionally!

"I first began prayerwalking when I moved to California. I had no friends, and I found myself walking alone on the beach, talking to the Lord. Today my friends (I met my Christian friends as a direct answer to one of the prayers prayed while prayerwalking!) and I zip down the beach path, praying together, praising God, petitioning him for our needs, speaking his Word, praying for others, and thanking him. Like Janet, we have been awed as we have seen the results of our prayers and discovered God's answers to these prayers as well as the benefits of being outdoors in God's beautiful world—improved physical and mental health."

—SUSAN WALES, author of *A Match Made in Heaven* and *Social Graces*

"Based on personal experience and not just on theory, *PrayerWalk* offers readers practical insights on how to get up, get moving, and get praying. The results can be life changing."

—ROBIN JONES GUNN, best-selling author of the Glenbrooke series

"Once in a while a book comes along that you just know is the book for 'such a time as this.' *PrayerWalk* is one of those. With depth and delight, Janet McHenry shares her adventures in prayerwalking, unveiling her struggles as well as her successes. Praying people everywhere will love this book and be changed by it. Those new at prayer will find it an invaluable resource. I highly recommend it!"

—TRICIA MCCARY RHODES, best-selling author of *Contemplating the Cross*

"Janet Holm McHenry brings the needs of mind, body, and spirit together in this wonderfully practical and encouraging book. Prayerwalking makes so much sense you'll wonder why you haven't been doing it all your life! A sincere, warm-hearted, and down-to-earth book, *PrayerWalk* is guaranteed to motivate and inspire."

—HEATHER *(The Dieter's Prayerbook)* AND DAVID KOPP, coauthors of the Praying the Bible series and *Praying for the World's 365 Most Influential People*

"Already a 'holy hiker,' I hoped *PrayerWalk* would offer new insights and hope to help me achieve greater consistency in prayer and exercise. I was not disappointed. Honest, humorous, and insightful, *PrayerWalk* will encourage your heart and help your hips!"

—LINDA DILLOW, author of *Intimate Issues* and *Calm My Anxious Heart*

"Men as well as women should read *PrayerWalk* because it contains great teaching on prayer as well as physical fitness. If you long for spiritual and physical fitness, this is the book you should read. Practical and real, *PrayerWalk* shows you what to do and why and has lots of encouraging stories and practical tips for how to make prayerwalking a lifestyle."

—ROGER C. PALMS, author of *An Unexpected Hope* and *Enjoying the Closeness of God*

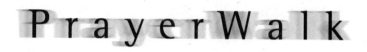

PrayerWalk

Becoming a Woman of Prayer, Strength, and Discipline

PrayerWalk

Janet Holm McHenry

WATERBROOK
PRESS

PRAYERWALK
PUBLISHED BY WATERBROOK PRESS
2375 Telstar Drive, Suite 160
Colorado Springs, Colorado 80920
A division of Random House, Inc.

Some of the stories in this book are composites of several different situations; details and names have been changed to protect identities.

Unless otherwise noted, scriptures are taken from the *Holy Bible, New International Version*®. NIV® Copyright © 1973, 1978, 1984 by International Bible Society. Used by permission of Zondervan Publishing House. All rights reserved. Scripture quotations marked (MSG) are taken from *The Message*. Copyright © by Eugene H. Peterson 1993, 1994, 1995. Used by permission of NavPress Publishing Group.

ISBN 1-57856-376-3

Copyright © 2001 by Janet Holm McHenry

Published in association with the literary agency of Janet Kobobel Grant, Books & Such, 3093 Maiden Lane, Altadena, CA 91001.

The author invites you to write her in care of WaterBrook Press.

All rights reserved. No part of this book may be reproduced or transmitted in any form or by any means, electronic or mechanical, including photocopying and recording, or by any information storage and retrieval system, without permission in writing from the publisher.

WATERBROOK and its deer design logo are registered trademarks of WaterBrook Press, a division of Random House, Inc.

Library of Congress Cataloging-in-Publication Data
McHenry, Janet Holm.
    Prayerwalk : becoming a woman of prayer, strength, and discipline / Janet Holm McHenry.
  — 1st ed.
     p. cm.
  ISBN 1-57856-376-3
    1. Christian women—Religious life. 2. Prayer—Christianity. 3. Walking—Religious aspects—Christianity. I. Title.

BV4527 .M393 2001

                                    00-043868

Printed in the United States of America
2001—First Edition

10 9 8 7 6 5 4 3 2 1

"To the only wise God be glory forever
through Jesus Christ! Amen."
Romans 16:27

———————

Also to my earthly father, Robert Arthur Holm, 1923–1999,
who loved to walk with me.
"I press on toward the goal to win the prize for which
God has called me heavenward in Christ Jesus."
Philippians 3:14

Contents

Acknowledgments

Many people have encouraged and supported me in countless ways from the conception of *Prayer Walk* until its birth. I am so grateful. Many thanks go to:

My husband, Craig, who has always encouraged me to do all God has called me to do—even prayerwalking at 5:00 A.M.!

Our children—Rebekah, Justin, Joshua, and Bethany—who are all on their own walks with God.

My Prayer Partners and One Heart sisters in Christ—forty-some strong—as well as my church family, who prayed me through this book word by word.

My agent and friend, Janet Kobobel Grant, who gave me sweet encouragement at just the right times.

My editor, Liz Heaney, who provided invaluable, wise direction, and all the WaterBrook folks, who saw the vision for *Prayer-Walk* and how it could change lives.

Since we live by the Spirit, let us keep
in step with the Spirit.

GALATIANS 5:25

Introduction

"You know I'm an ordinary Christian woman, God. But I'd like to become more disciplined, to have a consistent daily prayer time. I'd like to lose some weight and to be a little more fit. And…and…oh, this sounds crazy after everything I've just said, but I'd like to be content with my life."

This was my prayer two years ago. All of those requests and more have been realized in my life, all because of one thing: prayerwalking. Virtually overnight I changed from a woman who couldn't get out of bed to—Okay, I'm going to be brutally honest with you, dear reader. I am *still* an ordinary Christian woman. I probably look like the person in your high school class who was voted Most Likely to Become Your Kids' English Teacher, thirty years later. That's because that's exactly who I am! Let's just say you won't find my face and body on the cover of an exercise video. But God has truly changed me, and I am convinced it's because I now spend an hour or more five days a week praying as I walk. I call it prayerwalking—spending time with God in adoration and intercession as I walk the streets and highways of my community.

Stop right now! I know what you're thinking: *I don't have a free hour for prayer and exercise.* Hey, I don't either. It's true. If you were to examine my life, you'd see I don't have the time. I work full-time—teaching English, no less, which most secondary teachers agree is the most demanding position because of the mountains of writing assignments to grade. Craig and I have four children, with one still young enough to need Mommy's nearly constant attention. All have been active in sports, lessons, and other activities. I have a part-time business as a writer, I teach Sunday school, and I have very little housekeeping help. But I am *making* time for prayerwalking—an hour or more daily—because God has used it to transform me. I wrote this book to tell you, from my heart, how and why I started prayerwalking and the reasons I believe that if you make time for prayerwalking, God will change you as well.

Besides reading my personal story, you'll learn how you can pray more like Christ—our Personal Trainer in prayerwalking—and how prayerwalking can energize your prayer life. Prayerwalking has changed how I view my time and priorities, and I'll help you find time in your life for this new discipline. I'll also show you why walking while you pray is a good idea, and I'll provide a wealth of walking tips that can help prevent soreness before you head off on your own.

Join me as I share my story.

Part 1

Becoming a Woman of
Strength and Discipline

Chapter One

If I Can Do It, You Can Do It

Oh, that *d* word: *discipline*. I've never liked it, personally. We have met on occasion—with diets, short runs on exercise programs, and a prayer journal attempt or two. But life interfered with our acquaintance, and routines always fell by the wayside. Discipline implied torture, restriction, sameness. I mean, remember piano scales? Up and down, up and down. You never got anywhere, it appeared to me. Discipline simply stifled my spontaneity. Why, if I were committed to various routines of discipline, I couldn't visit a friend or take my daughter shopping or watch the ducks flying the wrong way.

I Was a Mess

Just two years ago I was falling apart. I bit my fingernails to their nubs with worry about finances (we had two kids in college). My weight was taxing my back, and my knees were giving way as I walked down stairs. I was force-feeding my soul with a few daily devotionals, but my prayer life was about zilch. Each night I gulped down a couple of St. John's Wort tablets to combat depression. I ate too much, I was tired all the time, and I felt as if I were a few days behind on every list of my life—from my load of essays at school to my laundry at home. I was an undisciplined mess.

I knew what I needed. I needed to exercise to get my strength back again. Could I exercise in the morning? I didn't really have time—I usually shut off the alarm around six each morning, exhausted, and turned over for an extra half-hour of rest, then rushed through my morning routine and headed to school an hour later. How could I give up even more sleep for exercise? With kids' sports schedules and lessons, faculty meetings, and few consistent baby-sitters, regular exercise after I taught school all day was impossible. There had been spells in my life when I was more active—aerobics and weightlifting classes, swimming laps at the pool. But classes always end, and our community pool is only open during the summer months. Besides, I didn't want to leave my kids once I was home from work.

I also needed to pray—at length—to give over the worries of my life to God. A book I read many years ago that still pierces me is *Could You Not Tarry One Hour?* by Larry Lea. Tarry an *hour?* It seemed like a Grand Canyon leap of time in my going-going-gone schedule. However, seeking God, interceding for others, and staying in his presence were becoming the deepest desires of my heart. I truly wanted to strengthen my relationship with the Lord of the universe by spending more alone time with him—without the phone ringing, without the kids interrupting, without the washing machine calling my name.

I've read over thirty books on prayer. Every single one recommends praying in the early morning hours. I had tried that over the years—getting up earlier than the family and creating my own prayer closet of sorts. Minutes into the routine, my head was usually flopping. You have probably guessed that I'm not a morning person. Actually, I'm not a night person either. I tell my high school students that most days I have one good hour—lunch hour (which is really only forty minutes for me)—and that afterward I'm ready for a nap. It's true!

However, I did stick to an early morning routine once. I thought of praying while I exercised, and for several months I propped my Bible on my NordicTrack and prayed through the Bible in the wee hours. That actually worked until my knees began to trouble me. Then the routine and I went our separate ways. My NordicTrack is now a great clothesline and keeps watch (wash?) in my office over my usually messy desk.

Two in One

I needed a workable plan, a resolution. I believe in New Year's resolutions, but my new year starts in September, when I return to teaching. All summer long I sleep a little later and mosey through my household chores and writing tasks. It's a leisurely pace. When school starts, I begin living by ringing bells again, so it makes sense to make my resolutions then.

When Labor Day passed that year, I felt pulled to become the woman of discipline I had never been. My past history could not have been a solid résumé for my success: Every day of my life seemingly had begun a new diet or a new exercise routine or a new prayer practice. Somehow my resolve that Sunday night in September felt different. I would do it this time. I would get up an hour earlier and tarry with God. Well, maybe *tarry* was not quite the right word because I had decided to spend my hour prayer-walking. I would walk for an hour, praying at the same time— meeting two sincere desires of my heart with one activity.

I loved the idea of doing two things at once. As a working mom, I always make multitasking a personal objective. Every morning I read the newspaper literally upside down as I lean over and blow dry my hair. I open my mail on the way home from the post office. I grade papers while listening to my daughter read at night. Although I may not be a model of organization, I love effi-ciency! Prayerwalking seemed a perfect solution to the two largest missing links in my life.

I had never before considered walking alone in the dark, early morning hours. The problem isn't that it's unsafe. In our town of just over a thousand people in a mountain valley in California, many not only leave their homes unlocked but keep their car keys in their ignitions. No, I'd not considered walking on Main Street because it didn't have sidewalks and because huge logging trucks sweep through on their way to the lumber mill. However, a few days before I made my resolution, brand-new sidewalks sculpted of brick and cement and brand-new lighting made our few blocks of downtown look like a fairy tale town. Elsewhere people walk in their local mall before opening hours. We have no mall in our town, but I decided that our half-dozen blocks of twinkly-lit Main Street would be my mall—my prayerwalking course.

Beating "The List"

At 5:20 the next morning I woke up moments before the alarm, turned it off, and rolled over. The List began speaking to me. "You're too tired; give yourself a few more minutes in bed." "It's probably too cold; why don't you walk this afternoon when the sun is out?" "Remember all those dogs? They're waiting for you!" "Bogeymen hide in the bushes!" "Your knee hurts; you'd better wait until you're in better shape." The List battered me for a few minutes until I remembered: I had not only made a physical-fitness resolution; I had also made a spiritual-fitness resolution.

Right then I realized that discipline involved another *d* word: *decision.* I could decide to be disciplined. I soon discovered that the decision to become disciplined had to be made daily (yet another *d* word.). Every single day I prayerwalked would be another decision, another step, toward discipline. That first day was no easier, no harder than any other. It was just a decision: Would I be a disciplined woman, for my own benefit, for the benefit of my family, and for the glory of God? I could not fix the physical and emotional pains of my life, but I could decide to meet God each morning while I walked.

After all, he wanted to be my Personal Trainer for becoming a woman of prayer, strength, and discipline. Some people have walking buddies. Others, like Oprah, pay someone to cheer them through a workout. I knew that in this new calling, prayerwalking, the Lord would be waiting at 5:30 on the front steps of my house, ready to hear my praise and petitions and to guide my steps—not only for the next hour but for the whole day ahead. How could I stay in bed when God was waiting for me? I got up! The first victory was won!

During my first months of prayerwalking I was too afraid I'd wimp out and jump back into bed if I undressed, so I pulled on lined nylon pants and a heavy sweatshirt right over my pajamas. As it grew colder, I added a coat, a double-layered knit hat, a woolen scarf, and gloves. Frost is our mountain manna about nine months of the year, and I've never liked being cold. I look pretty funny when I walk, but it's no fashion show at that hour, and I stay warm. Yes, it took a friend of mine several months to realize it was *I* walking early in the morning—he thought I was a guy with all the heavy clothes on.

I started out slowly. Although my enthusiasm was high, I knew that if I overdid my first days, I could risk injury and discouragement. I strolled down Main Street, then picked up the pace a bit. That first day I walked a mile and a half in a half-hour. I increased the distance over the next weeks until I was consistently walking three miles in an hour. (Now I walk five miles in less than an hour and a half—fives times a week.)

Changed!

I had thought that I'd be alone with God that early morning hour. At first I devoted the entire hour to prayers for my husband, Craig, and for our four children, Rebekah and Justin, both away at college, and Joshua and Bethany, who are still at home. But one morning a couple of weeks into my prayerwalking changed all that. As I approached Toddler Towers, our local day-care center, two cars drove up from opposite directions and parked, almost in sync. In one I recognized my friend Cheryl, ready to open the home-away-from-home for a couple dozen little ones. Emerging from the other, a young father swept up his curly-haired little girl, still in jammies and holding her blankie, and handed his sleepy package to Cheryl. I was okay until the bundle said, "Bye, Daddy. Love you." When I heard those words, the immenseness of my prayer job hit me. My prayerwalk was not just for my family and myself, but also for the many others I would encounter on Main Street. I began to cry—*bawl* is a better word. I cried and prayed for all the little children and their mommies and daddies, as well as the day-care workers who would mother and teach the children that day.

On subsequent days my Personal Trainer opened my eyes to other needs along my path, and I added new prayers. As I passed my church, just a half-block off Main Street, I prayed for our board members, who were desperately seeking direction. I prayed for the other two churches in town, which had their own struggles. I prayed for the owners of the businesses I passed each day, the principals and teachers at our three schools, the commuters leaving early for hour-away Reno, and the men heading for the day shift at the lumber mill. I added the city council members and the county supervisors and other government workers. Soon I discovered a sober truth: I didn't have enough time to pray for all the needs.

The experience was not only sobering but had another effect.

One morning about two months after I began prayerwalking, my younger son, Joshua, then thirteen, came into the kitchen and said, "What are you doing, Mom?"

I looked down at the counter and back at him. Maybe he didn't have his contacts in. "Making peanut butter sandwiches?"

"No, Mom," he said accusingly, "you were *singing*." He walked away, shaking his head.

He was right. I *was* singing. I, the one whose usual morning words were only *Get up...I said get up...Get up or you'll be late*—and other variations on the same theme—was singing. God had been filling my soul while I prayerwalked, and I couldn't hold it in anymore. It occurred to me that my entire countenance—in fact, my entire outlook on life—had changed. Prayerwalking an hour each weekday had transformed my life—in just a couple of short months.

On an ordinary morning I made the decision to prayerwalk. On an ordinary morning you could do the same and thus change your life in similarly dramatic ways. Walk with me. Walk with me over city streets, small town paths, and country roads. Let me show you how one daily decision can make a difference for our world. Walk with me through joys and sorrows, through hopes and fears, through laughter and tears. Let me show you how talking with God each day will be better than extra sleep. Decide to seek a healthier lifestyle, and let me prove that "discipline" can actually feel good. Join me and our Personal Trainer...and prayerwalk your way to physical and spiritual strength.

Chapter Two

Spiritual Endorphins

For most of my Christian life I thought there was something deeply wrong with me. I was raised in a Christian, churchgoing home and made a commitment to follow God when I was in college. Even so, I have lived almost all of my adult life under a cloud of depression. I never understood lines from the Bible such as "the joy of the LORD is your strength" (Nehemiah 8:10) because I had never experienced joy. I had had fleeting moments of fun, happiness, or satisfaction, but I was not filled with joy.

I was a critical person. That made me a good editor—nitpicking all the grammatical errors when I worked for a newspaper. That also makes me a good English teacher—helping students go from writing a disorganized mess to something that makes sense. But my critical nature made me negative with my children, critical of their grades and their sports achievements. I always felt they could have tried harder. I nearly lost the love of my two oldest children, Rebekah and Justin, because of my critical eye and demanding nature. I was even more critical of myself. My best efforts at mothering and teaching lived under my own fault-finding scrutiny. I was a pusher, not a pray-er; I would force issues rather than wait for

God to resolve them. I know now this was due to my need to control; when you pray, you give over control to God and trust him for the results.

When Craig and I built our home, I wanted to fill it with pretty things. When the house was filled, I was ready to build a bigger and better home so I'd have space to get all the other things I decided I needed. I was never satisfied.

When I was pregnant with Joshua, our third child, I remember feeling particularly lonely. I longed for a phone call from a friend, but it seemed I had to initiate all contact with others. When I brought this up to a friend and asked her why she hadn't called, she told me, "Well, I guess I have been avoiding you because you're just kind of depressing to be with." Ouch!

It was true. Sometimes sadness would simply envelop me for no reason. I cried in closets. I drove away to nowhere in tears. I sat on my bathroom floor in the middle of the night, trying to rock away a very real hurt in my chest.

As a teacher I have referred for counseling countless students who have displayed symptoms such as mine, but I never sought help for myself. I should have, but I didn't. I was afraid that others would think I wasn't capable of teaching my friends' children or of leading activities at church. Perhaps publications wouldn't want to print my byline because they would see me as "unfit."

It's hard to write this, but I can't tell you how many times over the years I have wished that I were dead. I should have bought stock in a tissue company years ago for all the boxes I have emptied wiping away my tears. Despite my despair, I knew I would never put an end to my life. I have personally lived through the suicide of six people—one of my best high school friends, a friend from a church couples' group, two fathers of my students, two youth in our church who were children of our friends. I would not do that to my family. But the pain of living was sometimes overwhelming.

The Cloud Vanishes

The miracle of my life is that three months after I began prayer-walking, my depression was gone, and it has not returned. I recounted in the first chapter about the moment I realized that—when my son found me singing, in the *morning* for goodness' sake. Although I am still groggy when I awaken, I get up now with a sense of expectancy. *What will you do today, Lord?* I wonder. *What crazy thing will some student say? What delightful drawing or observation will Bethany bring home from school? How will I live out my faith in my public school in such a way that my life makes a difference to someone?*

I notice things, too, now—details I missed before: the patterned pinpricks of light in the dark sky above our mountains, the color changes of the sky in the morning (I love how the black changes to blue so gradually), the way autumn smells sweet like something fermenting. And sounds! Our town's aspens resemble a baby rattle in a soft wind. Have you ever noticed how water doesn't slide silently over rocks but rushes and slurps? I love walking on the bridge over the creek and hearing the water greet me each morning. At rare times the creek freezes over, but there's still a muffled whisper calling me from underneath the ice as I pass by. It's such a beautiful world.

Prayerwalking has changed my outlook on life. In years past, my husband, Craig, was the positive one of the two of us. When life threw mud, he'd make mud pies. I'd whine and complain and hold grudges, never getting over the mess. It's different now. Instead of obsessing, I tell myself, "Get over it!" Instead of despairing when I am shown the back side of the tapestry of life, I now trust that eventually I will see the beautiful side that God has woven.

When my students found out I was writing a book, they wanted to know the title. I told them about *PrayerWalk*, and after they worked through their shock that their middle-aged English teacher was writing a book related to exercise, they also wanted to know why I prayerwalked. I told them, "Hey, it's cheap therapy." You might laugh too, but think about it—it is!

Not only was I freed from depression, I was freed from fear as well.

Good-bye, Fear

When I started prayerwalking, my oldest two kids were both planted across the state in college. Rebekah was a sophomore at Biola University in LaMirada, which is smack in the middle of the Los Angeles area's mass of asphalt. Justin was starting at Cal Poly in San Luis Obispo, which ordinarily is a lovely community but at that time was plagued by several unsolved murders of young people. Much of my intercession time as I began prayerwalking revolved around their safety.

I suppose all mothers worry some. Perhaps it's in our genetic makeup. But my fears were beyond normal. When Craig and I would drive over winding roads, I was sure we'd plummet down mountainsides. I pictured bridges collapsing as we crossed. In the early years of our marriage, we lived in northeastern Kansas. For every bend of the road I had mapped out a refuge in case a tornado swept over that area of the Flint Hills. That may not seem too weird, but until recently I did the same here in our mountain valley, and there's no way a tornado would form here.

Prayerwalking challenged my fears. First, I was choosing to walk in the dark. Second, I don't like strange dogs. I've been attacked three times and bitten twice in our town. Third, we live in a rural area where wildlife often decides to penetrate our residential borders. Bears, mountain lions, coyotes, rattlesnakes, and other critters are spotted frequently here. (Remind me to tell you about the mountain lion near miss.) Oh, yes, skunks are around our house all the time.

For months I had to pray against the spirit of fear. When my heart would pound not from exercise but from fear, I would speak aloud something like this: "Fear, I speak to you in the name and in the authority of Jesus Christ. I am a child of the Most High God. In the name of Christ, who has conquered death, I tell you to leave me alone and to go to the place reserved for you." I would then immediately ask the Holy Spirit to fill me and protect me. In every single instance I experienced immediate peace and continued my prayerwalk.

Eventually, after about six months, I realized I was not experiencing fear in my life anymore. It was right after my dad died. In fact, losing my dad was one of my greatest fears. I couldn't imagine life without him. Who would give me daddy hugs and say, "I love you, darling"? Who would I be without a father?

Less than five months after Dad's diagnosis of Lou Gehrig's disease, I took some of my gifted and talented students to the Oregon Shakespeare Festival in Ashland, more than five hours away. I came home the next day to a message to rush to Sacramento, three hours away. The doctors didn't expect Dad to make it through the night. When I arrived, my brother Matt greeted me with outstretched arms. "He's with God! He's with God!" Though I know those words were meant to comfort me, suddenly I was faced with one of my greatest fears. My father was no longer with us—he was with God. My dad was gone.

The days that followed are a blur. Writing obituary after obituary for newspapers all over the country. Eating other people's food. Writing a testimonial for the service. Walking into a very pink funeral home. Looking at grass-covered plots and wondering how the earth could ever be big enough for my wonderful dad. Buying funeral clothes. That was particularly strange—when someone dies, you buy new clothes?

After many of the details were in place, I had to go home before the memorial service to care for my own family for a couple of days. I arrived just in time to see Joshua's basketball tournament game. I walked into the gym, met my friends with that we-know look on their faces, and found a seat in the midst of all of them. Although the game was fast-paced and exciting, it didn't for one moment remove the sense of overwhelming grief that fell over me. Once when I stood to cheer for my son, my legs gave way. I was so weakened by the events of the previous days I literally could not stand up. In that crowded room of cheering fans, I sat quietly and sobbed.

Two days later I returned to my mom's. When you're the oldest in the family, the others often look to you for guidance and support, but all I wanted to do was sleep. One morning about a week after Dad's death I realized that I hadn't prayerwalked in over a week. I decided I would that morning before I did anything else. Minutes later I was strolling down the country lane, reiterating my fears about losing Dad in sobbing pleas to my heavenly Father. Each new block, each new step, God reminded me that my ultimate protection, comfort, and identity all rest in him alone.

I am your refuge and strength.

My compassions never fail—they are new every morning.

I have chosen you and you are my child.[1]

I had always known that I was chosen by my heavenly Father, but for the first time in my life I needed to experience him as my father. As I prayerwalked, I began to understand that God the Father, the Great Creator and Sustainer of the whole universe, was also Abba, my daddy, who would be the one to protect me, to comfort me, to love me. Realizing this in no way discounted the love or value of my earthly father, Robert Holm. In fact, he was a wonderful earthly model of God's love. As I thought about it, I knew that my dad would urge me to accept his Creator's love and care for me, just as God mercifully loved and cared for my dad in his last days and hours.

God's peace flooded over me as I prayerwalked that morning. The grief was not gone; in fact I would struggle with it for a long time. But God's strength had supplanted my weakness. I was free from another dark cloud. Fear no longer has a grip on my soul. I don't know how to explain it except to say, "To God be the glory." He met me at the corner of one of my greatest fears, walked me through it, and saw me to the other side of it. Since that time I have not experienced paralyzing or obsessive fear. I am no longer afraid of the dark. I greet dogs when I meet them in the morning. I do not look out for bogeymen on every corner. The irrational fears are gone.

Fear Versus Caution

However, when I've prayed against fear and something still nags, *This isn't right,* I've learned to pay attention. Ours is a dangerous, wicked world. My community is a sleepy mountain town that might seem distant from big-city problems, but evil influences still creep in. Drugs bring down our youth. Alcohol destroys families. An independent spirit that may have originated in Gold Rush days still has an influence on those who would rather do their own pioneering thing than seek God's direction.

So I try to discern between fear and caution: God's caution doesn't go away. I've found that God will still tug on me, make me wonder, make me extra alert. I believe God can give us caution or even physical resistance when the path ahead is not safe. In Acts 16:6 the Spirit prevented Paul from traveling to Asia. I think God does similar things today.

Let me illustrate this principle with that mountain lion story I referred to earlier. One morning several months ago, as I opened the door, I grumbled. It was snowing, and I would be delayed for a couple of minutes while I changed into my snow boots. I also grabbed my umbrella. Outside, I playfully kicked through the fluffy inch that lay on the sidewalks. A hundred feet down the highway from my house I stopped, frozen. A large set of animal prints spread out in front of me, crossing the highway just past the minimart. They were elongated, not round like a dog's or a cat's or even a bear's. They were also smeared and inconsistent in pattern. I'd never seen anything like them. *A mountain lion's?* I placed my mittened hand over one of the prints; the track was several inches longer still.

Fear struck. Run! *No, you don't run from a mountain lion.* The animal had just been there—the tracks were still fresh in the snow. If I hadn't stopped to change into my boots, I probably would have seen it. *It must be hungry to come right into town…looking for easy prey. A cat, a dog…me?* I looked around and prayed against fear. My body immediately stopped shaking, and I even laughed at myself. I took a deep breath and continued on. Yes, the fear fled, but I must have looked a sight. Just for good measure, I decided to swing my open umbrella and sing "Amazing Grace." Really loudly. It had occurred to me that perhaps when God sent the angel to protect Daniel from the lions in the den, the lions' mouths were shut because the angel who kept Daniel company was singing stunningly beautiful music. All I know is that I didn't run into a mountain lion that morning. Perhaps he was running from my less-than-amazing music. Or perhaps he was afraid of a creature with a swinging appendage that looked very similar to a large, black umbrella.

A High That Lasts All Day Long

Experts would probably attribute the lifting of my depression and irrational fears solely to endorphins. Endorphins are small protein molecules, produced by our own bodies, that serve as neurotransmitters. During exercise they are released in large doses into the brain. *Endorphins* is short for endogenous morphines because they have a morphinelike effect, which means they can actually relieve physical pain. Endorphins also apparently control the body's response to stress, regulate intestinal contractions, and elevate mood. This natural opiate is what causes the "exercise high" that many people experience.

Throughout my life I have had periods in which I have exercised regularly. When I was in my twenties, I ran several times a week. When I was in my thirties, I swam laps. In my early forties I discovered the high school weightroom. I experienced the exercise high, but I still suffered from depression during those times. It was my ever-present companion, waiting for me when I fell off the endorphin mountain.

Believe me, prayerwalking gives me a different kind of high. I'm newly enthused about my job teaching high school English instead of ready to quit. The words "Mom, I got a speeding ticket" do not make me go ballistic. I challenge myself to come up with a joke rather than a sarcastic comment when gossip and negativity are permeating discussion. I simply have a confidence that God will work all things for good in my life. Certainly this is a turn-around from despair.

You see, my morning prayerwalk has centered my thinking for

the day on what God would have me do. I think God sends spiritual endorphins to my needy soul. I have dumped my emotional junk and the day's agenda on him, so I don't have to worry about the piles of ungraded essays or the latest unhappy parent of a student. I don't have to worry if we'll have enough money for the kids' tuition this semester or why my old van is making that new noise. I have forwarded my e-mail list of worries and fears to God and can delete the whole mess from my in-box. My Personal Trainer has become my companion, not only while coaching me as I prayer-walk but also throughout the rest of my day. What a difference!

Chapter Three

Making Time

As a teacher, I have tried to motivate my students in various ways. I think, however, that generally there are two types of people: Deciders and Feelers. Deciders are moved by logic: We think through a problem, figure out a solution that makes sense, and do it. Feelers are more moved by the heart: Emotion, circumstances, and other people sway them to decision. Fortunately, both types can be moved by prayer and God's Word. I don't think one type is quicker to move than the other. We just have different ways of evaluating a situation and making a change.

I mention this idea because as I was thinking about how to help you reorder your day and priorities to be able to prayerwalk, it occurred to me that not everyone is like me. I'm a Decider. "Just do it!" I always tell my Feeler-friend Judy. But what I haven't realized before is that "Just do it!" doesn't make sense to her; she has to feel the Holy Spirit moving her. God uses her emotions, while he uses my logic. What's really wonderful is that when I began to consider prayerwalking, God used both my logic and my emotions to move me. So, I think I can help both you Deciders and Feelers.

Fixing Your Eyes

Prayerwalking starts with the deepest of desires, the hungering for God. The day I started to prayerwalk, I wrote in my journal two quotes that I felt God was giving me for the year:

- "Be holy, because I am holy" (1 Peter 1:16).
- "Continually restate to yourself what the purpose of your life is. The destined end of man is not happiness, nor health, but holiness.... Never tolerate through sympathy with yourself or with others any practice that is not in keeping with a holy God."[1]

I wanted answers to prayer, but I also desired to become more like Christ. Paul tells us to fix our eyes not on what we see around us—the temporary things of this world—but on God. (See 2 Corinthians 4:18.) That's how I felt when I decided I wanted to pray more deeply and consistently. I wanted my eyes fixed on God, not the troubles and distractions of my daily life. I simply and sincerely wanted to know God more fully. I wanted the rest of my life to be different. I didn't want to get through a school day anymore and *then* think, "Oh yeah, hi, God." I wanted—I *still* want—to wear his presence from my home to my classroom to the teacher's room to my kids' ballgames and back home again. It was more than a logical goal or priority; it was the deep, deep desire of my heart. The eternal things of life had become more important to me than the external things.

Before you start prayerwalking, pray about it for a week or more. This is not another exercise program that you can try for a week or so and see if it's going to work. Deciders, meeting with

God regularly has to more than just make sense; it must be something you long for. Feelers, this must be a priority, or you'll find excuses for missing your appointments when you don't feel like it. We live in a world of distractions—good ones, even—so we must have our eyes fixed and purpose determined.

The Whole Coat

No matter what you are doing in your life's pursuits, you can find time to pray. I've been prayerwalking for two years, and I still don't like getting up at five in the morning. However, I have learned that I do have time for this spiritual exercise. During all those years when I claimed otherwise, I was wrong. I was also wrong when I thought I couldn't get up that early, and I was wrong when I thought the loss of sleep would be harmful.

When we give prayer a high priority, we do it. I resist the idea that we need to make time for prayer...that we find time to "fit God in." Scripture tells us that "In the *beginning* God..." (Genesis 1:1) and "In the *beginning* was the Word" (John 1:1). God didn't enter an already existing world, squeezing into a corner somewhere. The Creator existed before the created. The universe, even our daily universe, should center on him. Rather than thinking there are pockets in our coat of time where God can be accommodated, we need to see that the whole coat belongs to him. Every time I wake up and put it on, it's there because of him.

My day is full of choices. It may not seem like it, but every activity is a choice—a shower, my job, my overtime, a telephone call, my dinner making, bedtime. Although I usually move mechanically from one thing to the next, I am making choices. Right now I'm choosing to work on this book after teaching all day and attending an after-school meeting. I'm also choosing *not* to do a lot of things—reading a friend's new book or vacuuming my living room or planting my annuals or nagging Bethany to practice the piano (she's doing her homework quietly instead). Oops! Back again. Just then I was choosing to watch a thunderstorm move across our valley.

What we often forget to live out is the most important of the commandments: "Hear, O Israel, the Lord our God, the Lord is one. Love the Lord your God with all your heart and with all your soul and with all your mind and with all your strength" (Mark 12:29-30). As Christians, we are called to have different priorities. Jesus told a man, "Follow me," but the man said he needed to bury his father first. Jesus replied, "Let the dead bury their own dead, but you go and proclaim the kingdom of God" (Luke 9:60). He is telling the man that the spiritually dead can bury those who are physically dead; those who are spiritually alive should follow him.

Before you start prayerwalking, determine that you will put God first in your life. Developing a deep relationship with him will require time. Instead of looking for snatches of time, commit to meeting God regularly and faithfully, and then trust that the other choices of your day will be the right ones—because you have already chosen the Right One. You can still have your same job and your same work hours (unless he leads you otherwise), but God is now the number-one priority of your day, not a distant cousin met through e-mail once a month.

Garage Sales

My faith costs so little in my church-oriented small town, yet sometimes I don't want my faith to cost a thing. In fact, sometimes I seek payback. I want to "get something" out of the sermon. I want the songs we sing at church to meet my needs. I want a diversified program that a large church would have, even though we're only about one hundred or so souls on any Sunday morning.

As I first wrote this, my daughter Rebekah was sharing her faith in Turkey, a country that is 99.8 percent Muslim, which I find particularly ironic since many of the New Testament churches were established there. There is such a high cost for believing in Christ there that Turkish Christians often do not meet together. The bodies of ten new believers, in fact, were found alongside roads during the time she visited. I know nothing of that kind of cost for believing in Christ.

I have promised you a "two-fer" deal—that you will reap both physical and spiritual benefits from one exercise. But in your quest to become a disciplined woman of Christ, you may have to give up something. Jesus teaches that our faith is connected with sacrifice. In fact, I think he wants us to have regular garage sales. Christ tells us not to store up for ourselves treasures on earth but to store up treasures in heaven, "For where your treasure is, there your heart will be also" (Matthew 6:21). He compares the kingdom of heaven to a merchant who finds a pearl of great value and sells everything he has so he can buy it (Matthew 13:45-46). He answers Peter's question about what will be in heaven for the disciples, "And everyone who has left houses or brothers or sisters or father or mother or children or fields for my sake will receive a hundred times as much and will inherit eternal life" (Matthew 19:29). If I'm not regularly holding spiritual garage sales to give up spaces of my life, then I'm not sincere in my desire to know Christ more fully.

This next step, then, is having the willingness to give up something. You probably know of this sacrifice; something has to give when you're doing ministry for others. If you serve on an advisory board, you give up hours with your family for evening meetings. If you have a gift for giving, you sacrifice some of your financial resources. If your gift is hospitality, you relinquish the privacy of your home to meet others' needs. Similarly, prayerwalking is ministry. Interceding for others is ministry. You may have to give of your time and strength and even some of your favorite activities to fulfill this call to pray. You may have to spend less time accumulating and caring for material objects. You may have to give up a hobby you love—a pearl of sorts that takes up your hours. However, because prayerwalking is all about relationship building with the Lord of the universe, ultimately those hours will be more satisfying than anything else you can imagine.

We cannot do all that we'd like to do. We have to make choices. Sure, Christians should be active in the world, but our orientation toward life should be different. We place God first in our lives and then discern how he would fill the rest of our hours. A lot of this requires understanding the concept of calling. If God has called you Deciders to pray, you'll find that something else just doesn't make sense anymore. You Feelers may find that another activity of your normal day isn't as joy-filled. But both of you will be able to let that thing go. Always pray before you follow purely human logic or feeling, then follow through with God's leading.

Some sacrifices could be

- giving up late night or early morning television
- cutting back on reading
- talking less on the phone
- spending less time on the Internet
- changing a focus from shopping (browsing as a leisure activity) to task-oriented errand running
- skipping coffee and tea breaks
- limiting evening commitments or stipulating that you can only stay until a certain time

Ideas for prayerwalking times are listed later in this chapter. These ideas are just to help you see that you can make sacrifices.

God Calling

Part of your sacrifice may involve letting someone else down who normally counts on you. Just this week I had to tell a friend that I couldn't attend a women's fellowship she was starting one night a month. I could hear the edge of hurt in her voice when I tried to explain that I don't do regular evenings out. I was sure she was thinking, *But it's just one night a month!* In the same week I tried to explain to a church board member why I wouldn't be attending the new weekly prayer meetings. I'm sure he was even a little miffed, since the prayer time largely gained momentum from a prayer conference I had organized. He was probably thinking, *But it's just one night a week!*

You can't expect others to understand what your calling is.

That's between God and you. However, ultimately you will only have peace by following *God's* leading—not what others, even Christian men and women, think you should be doing. So part of your sacrifice may be that others feel you're letting them down in their efforts to do the ministry to which God has called them.

Improving Your Posture

Like me, you may need to learn how to slow down to spend more time with God. Mary of Bethany shows us how to fix our eyes on Christ. It is the winter of A.D. 29 when her sister, Martha, invites Jesus into the home they share with their brother Lazarus (Luke 10:38-42). This is the last full calendar year of Jesus' ministry on earth. It started with the beheading of John the Baptist and continued with ministry in Galilee—healings and two miraculous feedings of thousands. Then Jesus' brothers urged him to go to Jerusalem, where he faced continual challenges and conspiracies against his life. He must have been relieved to receive Martha's invitation to their home in Bethany, two miles east of Jerusalem. In the sanctuary of their home Jesus could rest.

As he speaks, Mary sits at his feet and listens to him, while Martha is distracted by preparations that have to be made. Martha is perturbed when Mary doesn't help her prepare the food. She wants Jesus to scold Mary and asks him, "Lord, don't you care that my sister has left me to do the work by myself? Tell her to help me!"

Jesus replies, "Martha, Martha, you are worried and upset about many things, but only one thing is needed. Mary has chosen what is better, and it will not be taken away from her."

Martha is described as "distracted" by what she perceived was needed for the guest, Jesus. The Greek word that is translated *distracted* means to be pulled away or to be pulled apart. Those things that she perceived as important—fixing good food and preparing sleeping accommodations—pulled her away from her guest.

Perhaps you've been invited to dinner by someone like Martha. Everything was perfectly sumptuous, but you hardly got to spend a minute with your hostess because she was too worried about how to impress you—fixing elaborate dishes, changing the music, picking up her teenager's Hansel and Gretel trail from the front door to his bedroom. You see, what made you uncomfortable, perhaps even peeved, is that *you* were the reason for this event, but you were ignored.

As you determine to deepen your relationship with God, you'll also need to recognize when to set aside the urgent so that the important can be done. We can't ask Christ to dwell inside our hearts but fail to give him the time of day. Conversing with the Guest will require slowing down. You wouldn't say, "Sure, come on in, make yourself at home," and then go on with your regular activities. Sure, Jesus was hungry, but Martha didn't understand that it was more important for him to feed her than for her to feed him. I see prayerwalking as my choice to sit at Jesus' feet for an hour or so every day.

Praying Solitaire

So how do we un-busy our lives? My former title was Queen Busy Bee. When I was in my senior year of high school, I held six offices, including newspaper editor and youth group leader. My life didn't slow in my early adult years. One Easter morning years ago I sang a solo at the sunrise service, fixed and served the breakfast afterward for worshipers from two churches, taught a junior church lesson, sang in the choir during regular worship, and had a dozen folks over for a ham dinner. I mean, my middle name should be Martha.

It always seems as though we *have* to be on the go. This was true for Martha, too: The "preparations that had to be made" kept Martha from sitting at Jesus' feet (Luke 10:40). The Greek word used here is *diakonia,* which means service or ministry. It's used in the New Testament both for domestic duties, as in the passage in Luke, but also for spiritual ministration. The problem for us Christians is that we often can get so entrenched and busied by many good things—even things done in Christ's name—that these good things actually distract us from the Lord and what he would want us to do. Joanna Weaver in her book *Having a Mary Heart in a Martha World* quotes Dutch Sheets, who calls this a "treadmill anointing."[2] Let's not get so involved in ministry that we forget The Minister.

But let's also not beat ourselves up over this orientation. Even Jesus was challenged by "do-gooding." In Mark 1 he begins his first preaching tour through Galilee. While teaching at the synagogue in Capernaum, he is confronted by an evil spirit inhabiting a man. Jesus heals the man, and word spreads quickly throughout the whole region. Later that same day Jesus healed Peter's mother-in-law of a fever. That night the whole town showed up to be healed. Now, have you ever gone to the doctor's office or emergency room with a sick or injured kid? I have, dozens of times. Usually there are several people in line before us but not the whole town. Can you imagine the stress a doctor would feel if the whole town showed up without appointments?

The next morning Jesus got up while it was still dark and went out to a deserted place to pray. When Peter and friends found him, he said it was time to move on "so I can preach there also. *That* is why I have come" (verse 38, emphasis mine). His time in prayer evidently helped solidify his God-given purpose. The next verse tells us he traveled throughout Galilee, proclaiming the message in synagogues. Yes, he continued to heal, but in the shadow of the greater ministry, proclaiming the good news of eternal life through faith.

When you begin putting God first in your life, you will find that he does not call you to do good for the sake of do-gooding. When you serve, it should be for God's glory, not for your own praise. When God leads us to meet others' needs, we respond out of obedience, not because others think we should. We do not have to do all things. We do not have to be on church committees and in the choir and at the weekly meetings. Our children don't have to do all things either.

"But you don't understand!" you argue. "It's my kids' fault. Each only has an interest or two, but we're always running in opposite directions!"

Ah, yes, I answer, remembering the days when Craig and I wondered how we were going to get three kids to ball games in three different towns at the same time. Hindsight can provide a little insight. If you're in the ball game season of life, you may have to give up some of the things you love to do so that your kids can do their thing. However, as Christian women we are not to wear ourselves out while we neglect our relationship with God. A commitment to prayerwalk will likely mean a different fashioning of your day, your week. But it will all be worth it. I do not for an instant regret any time I have spent in prayerwalking on my community's streets.

Got Time?

In an article in *Walking* magazine, actress Jamie Luner says, "If you've got time to sit in front of the television, to go out to dinner with your friends, or to read a book, you've got time to work out and take care of yourself."[3] I'd like to revise that: If you've got time for those activities, you've got time to prayerwalk.

Are you ready to make time? If so, then here's how to begin.

Take a realistic look at your daily schedule and decide when to prayerwalk. I knew I would not be able to consistently prayerwalk in the afternoon. I have faculty meetings, kids' lessons and games, doctor appointments, and the like, which kill off free time before dinner. Evenings wouldn't work either; Craig, my husband, works late farm hours a lot of the time, and he wouldn't be home to watch our youngest.

I also felt my family should not have to sacrifice because *I* had made the decision to spend time in prayer. It was my ministry, not theirs. I didn't feel it would be appropriate to ask them to give up something simply because I had to do this new thing that would complicate their lives. It had to be my sacrifice. I wouldn't leave my daughter in day care after school. I wouldn't leave the others home during the dinner hour or the family time after dinner. I wouldn't leave Craig stranded after the kids had settled down to bed, even though that had been a favorite exercise time of mine over the years. No one, however, misses me during the wee morning hours. My sleepyheads are all snoozing away. Clearly, the best time for me to prayerwalk is first thing the morning.

Prepare ahead of time for your prayerwalking schedule. Because I know I'm going to meet God each weekday morning at five o'clock, I prepare the night before—getting my kids to bed on time, finishing my chores early in the evening, saying no to outside evening activities, settling myself down to my own Bible study routine, and turning off the light at a decent time. It would be easy to stay up late with my night-owl husband, watching old movies. However, prayerwalking demands many noes in my life, so that I can say yes to God.

If you work outside the home, one of the following ideas may help you see how you can meet God regularly:

- Go to bed sooner, and get up earlier.
- Prayerwalk your way to work instead of driving or taking public transportation.
- Combine your morning and afternoon break times and prayerwalk near your business.
- Prayerwalk during your lunch hour. This could be a good time of prayer fellowship with a work partner.
- If you have flexible hours, negotiate a shorter lunchtime on some days, so you can prayerwalk on others.

- Enlist family help for chores so evening hours are freer.
- Enlist husband or kids to empty the dishwasher in the morning, pack lunches, and make breakfast.
- If you carpool to work, have your carpool friend drop you off within walking distance of your home on days you don't drive.
- If you belong to an exercise spa, cancel your membership and prayerwalk instead.
- Prayerwalk while your kids are at lessons or ball practices. I have prayerwalked while my daughter was at piano lessons and at soccer practice.

For women who work at home, particularly those who have small children or who homeschool, here are additional suggestions:

- Organize a cooperative with other mothers—playgroups or curricular study groups—in order to rotate some free time.
- See if your spouse can come home for lunch while you prayerwalk.
- Ask a neighbor to watch your children while they're napping.
- Ask Grandma or Grandpa to do a regular story or game time.
- If family is not nearby, perhaps your church has a senior mentorship program that provides for pairing of senior folks with young people.
- Take your kids strolling for naptime. Jogger strollers are easier to push, and while they're a little expensive, sometimes they can be found at used children's clothing stores or garage sales.

- Prayerwalk around your local park while your kids play. During the summer when I don't have to teach, I drop Bethany off at our local pool on weekday mornings for swim team practice. Then I head down the country road for a solid hour and a half. We both get to do something we love, and we have the rest of the day together.

"I Only Have Eyes for You"

As I said earlier, I didn't want to fill this chapter with time-management suggestions. Plenty of books are devoted solely to that subject. I don't want to encourage you to "fit God into" your life but to help you center your life on him. I have chosen the first part of my day for regularly meeting him, but Jesus used various times of day for seeking out the Father: early morning (Mark 1:35), daytime (Matthew 14:13) and evening (Matthew 14:23). The important thing is that you choose a time when you can be faithfully consistent, so prayerwalking becomes part of the pattern of your life. Sleep, eat, prayerwalk—that sort of thing.

Do I ever miss a day prayerwalking? Yes. Either a child is sick or I am. The weather looks threatening. One time I prayed through most of the night for a friend who had lost his mother, and I was too exhausted to get up a couple of hours later. And sometimes, friend, I simply fail. When the alarm rings, once in a while I tell myself I'll get up in "just a minute or so" but reawake with barely enough time to make it to work. On those days I try to reschedule my prayerwalking appointment for later in the day. Or I try to find time over the weekend to meet God alone.

My Personal Trainer's office hours are twenty-four hours a day—and I don't even have to have an appointment! He walks with me into my classroom and reminds me to pray for my students. He helps me keep my mouth shut in the faculty room when I'd like to join in the gossip. He gives me insight in meetings with parents—to know what the root problem is and how to respond. I feel I am a more effective teacher because I prayerwalk on my workdays.

As you fix your eyes on Christ, you will be a more effective, more disciplined woman of God as well. The most important time of your day will be that half-hour or more that you have walked with God. That's because, you see, you cannot commit yourself to a life of prayer and remain the same. In time your sacrifices, like mine, will begin to seem meager compared to the huge dividends God is paying in your life and others' lives.

Recently I've been humming a favorite song, "I Only Have Eyes for You," because it reminds me of my life's new focus: "But GOD, dear Lord, I only have eyes for you" (Psalm 141:8, MSG).

Chapter Four

Why Walk?

I have had an achy back for a long time—from several falls down our stairs and a car accident years ago. In the weeks preceding my initial prayerwalks, my knees were giving way, my joints were aching so much I needed painkillers, and my whole body was stiff and inflexible. I also worried that my weight and inactivity could trigger diabetes, which had found its way into two generations preceding mine. I realize that every day I live brings me closer to the day I die, but I literally felt as though I were dying, with my body degenerating. I needed to exercise.

Here Are the Facts, Ma'am

As our society becomes more technological, our lives are increasingly becoming more sedentary. According to the U.S. Centers for Disease Control and Prevention, more than 60 percent of the adults in our country do not engage in the recommended amount of physical activity, and about 25 percent of adults in the United States are inactive. Millions of Americans suffer from illnesses that can be prevented or improved through regular physical activity, including 13.5 million with coronary heart disease and 8 million with adult-onset diabetes.[1]

Women are less physically active than men. As the mom of four kids who also works outside the home and is sitting at a computer at this moment, I nod my head when I read those statistics. It's hard to get out when you have children and are living a balancing act. But we need to do it.

What's So Great About Walking?

Most health-related organizations, including the American Heart Association (AHA), recommend vigorous physical activity for at least thirty minutes at a time, three to four days each week. The AHA doesn't limit its recommendation to walking, but I recommend it as the vehicle for prayer for three reasons. First, it's simple. You don't need an in-shape body; you can start out just as you are and build up to longer distances and intensity. Second, it's *simple*. You don't need elaborate equipment, just a good pair of walking shoes. Third, it's, yes, SIMPLE. You don't need to concentrate on what your body is doing; you can focus on God instead.

Some friends and family have joked about what my next book might be—prayerswimming or prayerbiking or prayerwhatevering. Believe me, I've tried praying while swimming laps and performing other physical activities, but I've literally hit the (pool) wall. It's hard to get the focus off myself and my breathing and the my-ness during other exercise activities. Many in my family are avid golfers, including my brother, Matt, who is a golf professional. He and Mom say they pray regularly when they play—probably something like this: "Please, God! Help me get the ball *over* the water!" Some sports may inspire prayer, but I'll stick to walking.

The Payoff

There are countless other reasons to walk while we pray. Many of them relate to physical benefits.

Walking Reduces the Risk of Dying Prematurely from Heart Disease

Regular exercise—including walking—is good for the heart. A study by a Boston hospital, conducted over a period of eight years and published by the *New England Journal of Medicine,* shows that brisk walking is associated with substantial declines in the incidence of coronary problems in women.[2] The American Heart Association writes that regular exercise can reduce or eliminate high blood pressure. It can also increase levels of HDL (a protein that carries good cholesterol in the blood); low levels of HDL have been linked to increased risk of coronary artery disease, so increased levels reduce that risk.[3]

It Reduces the Risk of Developing Diabetes

When my grandfather was my age, he contracted diabetes. When my mother was my age, she did also. At one point she was taking the full dose of insulin daily, struggling to keep her blood sugar in check. I often feel the blood sugar highs and lows that accompany the ebb and flow of my daily diet, so I ask my doctor regularly for the blood tests that screen for diabetes. So far, so good, but family history of this disease was an important factor in getting me to walk.

A Harvard study found that women who take a brisk walk each day can cut almost in half their risk of developing Type II diabetes.[4] The study reinforces the position of the Centers for Disease Control and Prevention and the National Institutes of Health, which, like others, advises that we should have at least thirty minutes of moderate intensity exercise daily. The study also says that walking is the exercise of choice because of its accessibility, ease, and rare association with injury.

It Helps Build and Maintain Healthy Bones, Muscles, and Joints

Walking can also help build bones. Bone naturally becomes thinner as we age, but women are particularly vulnerable here, often developing osteoporosis, which is the loss of protein matrix tissue from bone, causing it to become brittle and easily fractured. The disorder can advance more quickly after menopause, when our bodies stop producing estrogen, which helps maintain bone mass, or after removal of the ovaries.

With the expansion of the soft-drink industry in recent decades, women have also been drinking less milk, depriving their bodies of the calcium their bones need. The American Medical Association recommends walking to build bones but says that anything less than three brisk three-mile walks per week—or the equivalent—is not likely to help much when it comes to our bones.

It Reduces the Risk of Breast Cancer

A study reported by the Women's Health Information Center shows that women between the ages of thirty and fifty-five years can reduce breast cancer risk by 20 percent by exercising one hour each day. When the exercise is cut in half, the reduction of risk is also cut in half.[5]

My family doesn't have a history of breast cancer, but that doesn't make me exempt. I certainly know women who had no family history but have been struck by the disease. If we could take a pill that would lower the risk of breast cancer by 20 percent, most women would take it. It seems smart, then, to prayerwalk and get the same benefit.

It Combats Obesity

Walking burns about the same number of calories per mile as running does. According to the President's Council on Physical Fitness, a mile walked in fifteen minutes (yes, that's brisk!) burns about the same number of calories as jogging that distance in eight and a half minutes.[6]

I hesitate to suggest walking as the sole means to control weight, as it can become an obsession. I have friends who "must" run, even though they don't enjoy it. Instead of food controlling them, now exercise controls them. They look great, but in their hearts they know that another substitute for God has been made.

If you are struggling with weight-control issues, walking will help to some degree, but the answer to your problem is not another obsession. God is. Instead of running to food or running to exercise or running to the newest weight-loss fad, I strongly recommend that you read *Reasonably Thin* by Jesse Dillinger; its thirty-seven chapters walk you through strong Christian therapy on eating disorders. In the meantime, prayerwalking will help you get your focus on God in all areas of your life, diet included.

And that's not all. According to the Centers for Disease Control and Prevention, regular physical exercise performed most days of the week will also

- reduce the risk of dying prematurely
- reduce the risk of developing high blood pressure
- help reduce blood pressure in those who already have high blood pressure
- reduce the risk of developing colon cancer[7]

Three Health-Related Questions

Anyone who is over fifty or has high-blood pressure or respiratory or cardiovascular problems should consult a doctor before beginning a walking program. However, if you have not been exercising regularly, it's always wise to seek the advice of your doctor before you begin any exercise program—including prayerwalking. You and your doctor know best what you can and cannot do.

With that said, let me address three questions I hear a lot when I talk with women about prayerwalking.

What If I'm Sick?
My general rule is that if I'm running a fever or if I plan to stay home from work, I stay in bed. My first year of prayerwalking was the healthiest I had had in years. I only had two colds, and they were short-lived. I have been completely healthy this second season of prayerwalking.

The American College of Sports Medicine indicates that most Americans suffer from one to six colds per year and are able to fight them off whether they exercise or not. Research published in its magazine indicates that moderate exercise during a rhinovirus-caused cold does not appear to affect symptom severity or duration. Athletes who were inoculated with a rhinovirus and who continued to exercise had colds for the same duration as those athletes in the study who discontinued their exercise.[8]

The authors of that study recommend that if you are experiencing only a runny nose, sneezing, or a scratchy throat (above-the-neck symptoms), it's probably safe to begin exercising at a lower intensity and to increase intensity when the symptoms recede. If you have below-the-neck symptoms, such as fever, sore muscles or joints, vomiting, diarrhea, or a productive cough, you should allow the illness to run its course and then begin exercise when the symptoms are gone. I agree, and I think you'll find that beginning a regular prayerwalking discipline will decrease the risk that you'll even acquire an upper-respiratory infection. You'll be healthier than you've ever been.

What If I'm Pregnant?

If you were fit before you became pregnant, you can safely exercise moderately if your doctor has indicated you have a low-risk pregnancy. If you have previously not walked regularly, start out slowly, and be sure to ask your doctor about recommended levels of exercise.

While most pregnant women can maintain their exercise program throughout the nine months, the American College of

Obstetricians and Gynecologists (ACOG) states that some women should not exercise while pregnant. This group includes those who have experienced preterm labor in their present or a previous pregnancy and women who have obstetrical complications, including persistent vaginal bleeding, incompetent cervix, ruptured membranes, or a fetus who is not meeting expected growth intervals.[9]

Your physician should also approve walking if you have a history of high blood pressure, diabetes, heart disease, or thyroid disease. At this time there is no evidence that exercise has any negative effects on the baby or that it can increase the risk of miscarriage or birth defects. Studies have shown that exercise could lower a baby's birth weight, but this is attributed to a lower percentage of body fat; these babies remained in the average range for weight. Predictably, pregnant women who exercise may recover more quickly after the baby's birth.

Walking is one of three activities recommended by the American College of Obstetricians and Gynecologists for pregnant women beginning an exercise program. (Swimming and cycling on a stationary bicycle are the others.) The ACOG offers these exercise guidelines for a pregnant woman whose doctor has approved exercise during her pregnancy:

- Stop exercising when you begin to feel fatigued, and stop exercising immediately if you become breathless, dizzy, headachy, weak, or nauseous or if you experience chest pain or tightness, uterine contractions, or vaginal bleeding.
- Be aware that you have less oxygen available for exercise. Stop when you are fatigued, and do not exercise to exhaustion.

- Be aware that your balance can be affected, especially as you gain weight. I suggest that you be especially careful when approaching or leaving curbs or uneven walkways.
- Be sure to eat an adequate diet that allows you to gain twenty-five to thirty-five pounds over the nine months. Exercising will require that you eat more to maintain the weight gain.
- After the baby arrives, wait until your doctor approves your beginning a walking program.[10]

What If I'm in My Senior Years?

June, a longtime friend, and I have chatted on the phone nearly every day for years. When she started prayerwalking at age seventy-five, she'd usually tell me about each new ache. I told her, "June, I was so out of shape when I began, I ached for several months. My knees were snapping. My muscles were crying. My knees and shins and hip joints were screaming, 'Stop! We want to go home!'" She laughed and told me that maybe she didn't hurt that much after all.

Before you begin prayerwalking, seek your doctor's approval regarding walking. Researchers recommend large-muscle rhythmic and aerobic forms of exercise like walking for seniors. Walking in particular is recommended because it has been part of the older adult's life, and increasing it will probably not be a difficult lifestyle change.

Many people think they will inevitably slow down as they age. According to the American Association of Retired Persons (AARP), this is not true.[11] In fact, much of the physical frailty attributed to aging is actually the result of inactivity. It's possible to reverse the magnetic pull toward poor health by engaging in regular exercise.

Here are some specific recommendations, adapted from AARP's advice to seniors. (Chapter 5 has additional recommendations for beginning a prayerwalking discipline.)

- Begin with shorter prayerwalking sessions. Take rests as needed. Prayer need not stop with an exercise breather. God is still on the line, even when we hang up our tennies!

- Our balance may decline as we age. I also find that the multifocal lenses in my glasses make the earth "move" as I am looking down at the approaching curb. Choose an area with a smooth walking path.

- When muscles are not toned, unsteadiness can occur. A prayerwalking program should begin with realistic, achievable goals, which can be extended when the muscles are ready for longer commitments of time.

- Older folks may become dizzy if they stop abruptly. The blood needs time to return from the outermost parts of the body. (Notice how your hands swell when you're walking.) If you slow down gradually and end with some stretching, you'll avoid dizziness.[12]

Try It and See for Yourself

I have experienced dramatic physical changes since I started prayerwalking. I used to ache all over so much that I was crying myself to sleep at night. Sometimes painkillers wouldn't even take the edge off the pain in my hips and knees as I lay in bed rolling from one side to another, seeking the least painful position. All that is now gone, as well as extra weight, breathlessness with the slightest exertion, stiffness, and regular neck aches, backaches, and headaches. But I'm not the only one who has benefited from walking while I pray.

June says her doctor is happy that she is building muscle, maintaining bone mass, and keeping her weight down. She often suffers from insomnia but says prayerwalking helps her sleep better. "I walk for the sheer joy of planting one foot after the other on solid ground, for stretching out my legs, and swinging my arms. When I walk up the driveway and begin to stride along the way, I feel energized." June is my two-day-a-week partner who taught me to be thankful, as she says, "for the gift of walking." I had never thought of walking as a gift, but at seventy-six, she appreciates all her steps.

Friends Patti and Dena have also noticed dramatic midlife physical changes. As I write this, Dena is in her tenth week of freedom from smoking. Patti, who is losing weight, writes, "I have more discipline in eating and losing weight, and my blood pressure has dropped. It was borderline but now is no problem." She also reports that "Our attitudes and well-being have improved" and that "Overall we are a 'piece of work'—God's, that is."

Tricia, a young mother, told me, "I've not only lost weight, but I also don't get winded climbing the flight of stairs in my house." She has grown to love the outdoors more. "Not only do I look forward to walking in the morning, but almost every day I like to bike with my kids or hike with them in the woods behind our house. What a difference prayerwalking has made in my life!"

But don't take our word for it. Try prayerwalking for a while, and see what changes our Personal Trainer will bring about in your life.

Chapter Five

Reducing Aches and Pains

When I first started prayerwalking, I just headed out the door. I threw on some clothes and shoes and figured my Personal Trainer would pick up the pieces of my exercise decision. What ensued were complaining joints, a moaning back, and screaming shins. It's hard to sing about the joy of the Lord when the chorus is singing a different tune!

I'd like to help you begin your discipline better prepared than I was so that you can avoid the aches I let myself in for. As I wrote earlier, anyone starting a new exercise program should seek the advice of a medical doctor. She probably is not going to discourage you. Instead, you'll get some great guidance in case you have any health conditions that could be adversely affected.

Take Care of Those Feet!

One of the most important things you can do to avoid injury is to invest in a good pair of shoes. You don't want shoes with soles that are thick or highly elevated. Think about it: When you wear high-heeled shoes, what's the first thing you do when you get home? Take them off! They're not good for you. The same is true of some athletic shoes. When I first started walking, I stupidly wore the ones I had, which were actually basketball shoes. The lift and pockets in the heel threw off my posture and back alignment, and after a couple of months I was really achy, especially as I began increasing my intensity and distance. When I changed to a pair of running shoes, the aches disappeared.

Buy shoes that fit the shape of your feet and are comfortable from the moment you put them on. If your foot is wide at your toes and thin at your heels, your shoe should comfortably accommodate these features. Your foot should not slide around in the shoe; otherwise, you'll get blisters and corns. For a good fit, you should have a space the width of your thumbnail between the inside of the end of the shoe and your toes to allow for movement as you walk. Also, try both shoes on—it's not unusual for a person's feet to be different sizes. If this is the case, buy the size that comfortably accommodates the larger foot. (A second sock on the smaller foot may make that shoe fit better.) Lace the shoes snugly all the way up, and walk around the store a few times with them on. Don't rely on salespeople's advice or a brand name's image; only you know what feels good on your feet.

What Kind of Shoe Is Best?

There is much debate about this question. I have done a lot of reading on shoes and talked to several people who sell them. Some writers advocate that you should only wear walking shoes and say they are made with just the walker in mind. However, at least some of these folks are paid to endorse or sell walking shoe products. One retailer told me that walking shoes aren't much different than running shoes or cross trainers (shoes that can be used for both running and other sports activities). The only real difference is that walking shoes often have a leather outside covering.

Structurally, shoes specifically marketed for walking may have several features: a shorter heel than a running shoe, flexibility, extra cushioning in the heel and ball, and some structural features that may help keep the foot rock straight forward instead of rolling inward or outward. When shopping for a good walking shoe, check to see that the underside pad of the front of the shoe is flexible and whether the front of the shoe bends easily. It's okay to bend the shoe in the store—it should stand up to this. If you can easily bend the shoe into a U, it is flexible. When walking, you should land on your heel, rock forward, and push off your pad and toes. The shoes I'm currently wearing have a curved break across the ball area of the foot.

There are three kinds of running and walking shoes: comfort, support, and control. Before you decide which kind to buy, you need to know what kind of feet you have: pronator, supinator, or neutral. The function of each kind of shoe meets the needs of one of these three kinds of feet. Here's how to identify what kind of feet you have:

1. Place two pieces of dry construction paper on a hard floor surface.

2. Dampen your feet slightly.

3. Walk across the paper, leaving one foot pattern on each.

If you leave a large print of most of your foot, you are a *pronator*. That means you don't have much arch and your feet are somewhat flat. When you walk, your feet will roll inward. You can see this on the bottom of shoes you have worn for a while; they'll show more wear on the inside of the sole and will lean inwards.

If you leave little imprint on the paper—just the balls of your feet, toes, and heels—you are a *supinator*. You tend to roll your feet outward when you walk, because you have high arches. Your shoes will show wear on the soles' outside and will lean outward.

A support or control shoe will help correct your foot if you are a pronator or supinator.

If the imprint on the paper shows the toes, ball, outer outside, and heel, your feet may be *neutral*. The wear on the underside of your shoe will be even, and your shoes will lean neither outward or inward. If your feet are neutral, select a comfort shoe.

If your feet begin to hurt from walking, you should consult with a podiatrist. You may need to be fitted with customized orthotics for your shoes. When I first found out about these feet types, I took my shoes to a running store. The owner told me that from the wear on my shoes and the way they leaned in, he could tell I was a slight pronator. (I learned later that most people will pronate slightly.) If I experienced discomfort, he advised that I choose a shoe that provides support so my foot does not roll inward. But I have not experienced foot, back, or related problems since then, so my shoe that is designed for cushiony comfort seems to be all right for me.

What will these shoes cost? A fitted walking or running shoe in a specialty store or ordered through a catalog or the Internet will cost $80 to $120 or more. You can find a running shoe or cross trainer at discounted sports stores for as little as $40.

It's also advisable to replace them frequently. I need new ones about every five or six months. You should replace your walking shoes every five hundred miles—that's every six months if you're walking twenty miles per week. If you wear your shoes for anything other than prayerwalking, you need to add that additional wear into your calculation too. Take a look at the tread. Is it worn severely or uneven? Why take the risk of injury? Good shoes will be important to the health of your joints as you bang those hard surfaces. There are also safety concerns: I don't like slipping around on wet or otherwise slick surfaces. Allow yourself this one luxury as you prayerwalk.

No Fancy Gear Needed

The only other important clothing is socks. They need not be expensive. I found my favorite pairs at a discount store. I don't advise all-cotton socks; they can get soggy and saggy as you sweat and move. You'll want a blend of cotton, latex, and nylon or acrylic. They will cushion your feet, stay up, and keep the sweat away.

I didn't buy a single new piece of clothing for the purpose of prayerwalking. You won't need to either. You will eventually find some clothing more comfortable than others and some more practical than others, given certain weather conditions. A good sports bra is a smart investment. There are two types, the type that squishes you together and the type with separate cups. If you need extra support, you can wear the latter under the former.

Warm weather can provide challenges. I am blessed that I live in an area where I don't miss days prayerwalking because of the heat. During the summer (and daylight hours in general) the most important thing I wear is sunscreen. I wear a sweat-resistant lotion with spf 30. I love the freedom of wearing comfortable shorts and a modest scoop top when it's warmer.

The more challenging time for me is September to late April, when the temperature is often below freezing. That's a lot of cold over a year! I layer to stay warm. A top that is part cotton and part man-made fabric will help wick the sweat away from your body. On top of that add a loose sweatshirt, covered by a nylon jacket. I used to wear a heavy winter jacket with a cushiony fleece lining but found I could hardly move my arms and my motion was rather plodding. A nylon jacket lets me move more freely, effectively retains my natural body warmth, and keeps any wind from cooling me off. I wear Polartec tights (Land's End) underneath lined nylon pants. I also will start out with an acrylic scarf for my neck, a double-knit acrylic cap, and sometimes mittens or gloves. Mittens are more effective against cold. However, the sleeves of my nylon jacket are long enough to cover my hands, so even at about fifteen degrees, I often don't need a hand covering.

Many people tell me they don't walk in the winter because of the cold, but frankly, I don't start out cold, get cold, or end cold. If the temperature were near zero, I'd recommend the mall or your local high school gym, especially if there were even a whiff of wind. On rainy days I grab my umbrella and go anyway. (Do not, I should add, walk in strong wind or in a storm with lightning or hail.) On snowy days use boots. I have a pair of snow boots that give good support. If you have to walk regularly in snow or on trails, you might seek out special snow or hiking boots that are geared for walkers. You've heard about walking on water. Well, how about walking on ice? I have found a great product that allows me to continue prayerwalking on icy days: Get-a-Grip. They are rubberized fittings that stretch over your shoes, with small spikes on the bottoms so you won't slip on ice. They're available at running stores and cost about $30.

All walking authorities recommend drinking a lot of water while you walk. If, like me, you find there aren't enough bathroom stops on your route, or if you find that water bottles throw you off balance, drink tons of water when you get home. However, if you live in a warm climate, you'll need to carry and drink a lot of water. The rule is: If you are thirsty, your body is telling you that you should have had water sometime ago.

Some walkers use water reservoir devices available at bicycle shops. These devices allow you to thread a hose from the water reservoir on a waist pack up to near your mouth; you then just take a sip when you need one.

Some walkers also use devices such as ski poles (to increase the aerobic workout) or a cane (for steadiness), a flashlight, a heart-rate monitor, and a stopwatch or timer. I do not recommend that you walk with hand weights. I tried that for several months, working up to three-pound weights. I found that the weights really slowed me down and caused pain in my sternum area.

Monitor Your Heart Rate

If you want to walk as an aerobic exercise, you should learn how to monitor your resting heart rate and calculate your aerobic target range. But first, get your doctor's advice about what your aerobic level should be, given your age and resting heart rate and other health factors.

You can figure your own resting heart rate though. Put the first and second fingers of your left hand firmly against the left side of your neck, just under your jaw, to find your pulse. Count how many beats occur in a fifteen-second interval. Multiply that by four to get your resting heart rate. The American College of Sports Medicine provides an equation for figuring your aerobic target range. What this means is how fast your heart should beat to be considered at a safe, aerobic level. Here are the steps:

1. Subtract your age from 220.
2. Multiply this number by .5.
3. Also multiply the number from number 1 above by .75.

The numbers you get from numbers 2 and 3 above will give you the aerobic target range. For example, if I were forty years old, this would be my calculation:

$$220 - 40 = 180$$
$$180 \times 0.5 = 90$$
$$180 \times 0.75 = 135$$

My aerobic target range as a forty-year-old prayerwalker would be between 90 and 135 heartbeats per minute. Less than 90 beats per minute would probably not be considered aerobic; more than 135 beats per minute could be considered dangerous. Again, you can verify your target range with your doctor.

There are four types of walking.[1] Level 1 is lifestyle walking, like a stroll through a park or mall. Lifestyle walkers walk a mile in 17 to 24 minutes. This is a good entry level for you as you begin prayerwalking, particularly if you haven't been exercising. Level 2 is fitness walking. Fitness walkers move at the lower end of their aerobic target range, achieving a mile in 14 to 17 minutes. Level 3 is high-energy walking, which is at the upper end of that range. These race-walkers take a mile in 10 to 13.6 minutes, equivalent to the calorie burn of running. Level 4 is a combination of walking and running; you'd probably find that you were losing your prayer concentration at this level.

As you become fit, your aerobic range will move up. It will take more intensity to bring your body up to the aerobic level. My resting pulse rate is now 50 (I've been accused of being dead by nurses and doctors), about 10 beats slower than when I started prayer-walking. That means I need to walk at a more intense level to get aerobic benefits for my heart.

A simpler way to judge if you're in an aerobic mode is if you can't sing but can carry on a conversation. If it's your desire to prayerwalk at an aerobic level, you should work up to that intensity gradually as you also slowly increase distance. Give yourself time so as to avoid soreness or injury or discouragement.

Watch That Posture!

There are also proper posture and form for walking. To avoid back problems:

- Walk in a stand-up-straight posture with your eyes and chin facing forward. Don't lean your head or upper body forward; you'll get a backache.
- Bend your arms in ninety-degree angles and swing them back and forth—the right arm moving in sync with the left leg and the left arm in sync with the right leg.
- Your hands should be in a light fist; don't let them drag through the air, or your pace will also drag.
- As I mentioned earlier, your feet hit heel first and rock gradually to the ball and toes. (More complete information on walking form, as well as all other walking concerns, is available in the resources listed at the back of this book.)

What About Warming Up and Cooling Down?

There are several misconceptions about warming up, cooling down, and stretching. Some experts say stretching isn't important, and one writer says fewer than 20 percent of walkers stretch.[2] However, stretching makes your muscles more pliable and your joints and body just more flexible in general. I didn't stretch for over a year after I began walking and noticed too many aches and pains. After I began stretching, I began to enjoy freedom from those symptoms.

I used to think that stretching was a way to warm up. Not so.

You should not stretch before you exercise. When you stretch your muscles, tendons, and ligaments when they're cold and tight, you put too much stress on them. Warm them up first.

Warm up simply by walking at a slower pace for about five minutes or so, then work into the more aerobic levels. Some walking experts recommend stretching after about five minutes of walking, and you may prefer this. But I don't like to do my stretching routine out on the road somewhere, so I stretch when I'm done.

It's also important to cool down by slowing down at the end of your prayerwalk to the slower pace. An easy way to accelerate is by moving your arms faster; conversely, slow down by slowing down your arms. The rest of your body will follow.

Some Essential Stretches

It's good to stretch all your major muscle groups, including the hamstrings, calf muscles, quadriceps, buttocks, and inner thighs. I spend a good five minutes in my living room stretching out. Below are several stretches that are a must for the legs, and you may want to add additional ones for the upper body as well. Remember not to bounce when you stretch. Begin your stretching regimen with ten-second holds; increase to twenty- to thirty-second holds.

> **Hamstrings:** The hamstrings are the large muscles on the backside of your upper leg. Stretching them gives you a longer stride.
>
> *Stretch:* Stand with one heel on a sturdy chair, with toes pointing upward. Keep both legs straight and bend from the

waist, trying to touch your nose to your knee. This will also help strengthen the shins.

Calf muscles: The calf muscles are on the backside of your lower legs. These muscles are the major motors for your walking stride.

Stretch: You can exercise both upper calves with one stretch. From a distance of three to four feet from a wall, stand with your feet about a foot apart and your palms against the wall. Your body will lean into the wall.

Stretch: Stretch the lower calves and Achilles tendon by staying in the same position but with your knees bent slightly.

Quadriceps: The quads are your large muscles on the front upper thigh; you feel them when you're walking uphill.

Stretch: Reach down and grab your right ankle with your right hand, slowly pulling your heel up toward your buttocks while balancing yourself on your left leg. Repeat on other side.

Buttocks and outer hips: You may feel a tightness or soreness in these areas.

Stretch: Lie on your back. Put your right foot on your raised left knee. Pull your left knee toward you to feel a pull from your buttocks and hip. Repeat with the other side.

Inner thighs: If you haven't exercised much, you may also feel tightness in your inner thighs.

Stretch: Sit upright on the floor and put the soles of your shoeless feet together. Pull your feet as close as you can to your body, pressing down on your knees. Repeat a couple times. You can lean into the stretch but keep your back straight. This also will make your lower back and hips more flexible.

Shins: You may need a stretch of your shins when you start walking or increase intensity or distance.

Stretch: Standing or sitting, make a V with your right foot, with the heel alone on the floor. Stretch the toes toward you and hold. Repeat with the left foot. This can help relieve pain as you're walking.

Go for the Goal

Begin your walking program with a goal. To set your goal, answer the following questions:

- How many miles would you eventually like to walk each time?
- What maximum amount of time could you eventually devote to prayerwalking?
- What level of intensity would you like to reach?

To reach your goal, you need to realistically assess your current physical condition (again, with a doctor's advice). Then you can break down the ultimate goal into achievable daily goals. For example, if you hope to eventually walk four miles in an hour, this could be a workable plan:

- Give yourself a half-hour to walk one mile. This pace would be lifestyle walking—strolling.

- The next week, walk for ten more minutes, pick up the pace, and see if you can reach one and a half miles.
- Add intensity the next week and see if you can walk two miles in the forty minutes.
- Alternate adding minutes and intensity from week to week. You can expect some soreness when you start any exercise, but keep going unless the pain is severe. You can slow down your pace or cut back on distance a little to accommodate those aches, as needed.

I initially decided that I wanted to prayerwalk for an hour. I knew, however, that if I started with an hour, I could create stresses on my under-exercised body that could thwart my reaching this goal. I began by walking thirty minutes, then increased my time by five minutes a day and added intensity until I was walking my original goal of three miles in an hour. When I'm not walking with a partner, I now walk five miles in something under an hour and a half.

I decided to prayerwalk every weekday because I was afraid that if I only prayerwalked a couple times a week or every other day, I would procrastinate. I take off the weekends—Sunday for a Sabbath rest and Saturday for a husband rest.

I recommend that you set a goal of walking for at least a half-hour at least three times a week. Several books on walking offer scheduled plans for building up walking distance and intensity. I have listed several at the end of this book, along with my short reviews. Remember, if you're hoping to see physical changes (stronger bones, lower cholesterol, weight loss), you may want to eventually reach a walk of three miles at least three times a week at an aerobic level.

Remember the Focus

If a lot of the information in this chapter is new to you, it may feel as if these physical concerns could overtake our purpose of walking: prayer. However, all of the physical consciousness of walking will become unconscious after a few walks, and your focus will be on your Personal Trainer, not what your body is or isn't doing. I just think you'll be a little smarter than I was when I started if you take some of these suggestions to heart, particularly those that could prevent injury. The objective is to begin and continue a discipline of prayerwalking. If you go into the discipline carelessly, aches and pains could waylay you from your walk with God. And that walk, friend, is the ultimate goal.

Safety Precautions

- Walk with a partner.
- Walk in a safe area. Don't walk on a track alone; it may be too isolated.
- Face road traffic when you walk, using the very left side of the roadway.
- Look straight ahead at the approaching traffic, check all ways possible at corners before you cross, and never, ever challenge a car at an intersection or other point. Let the car win.

- At night walk in a lighted area and wear reflective material on your shoes and clothing. It's available in sports stores.
- Carry personal identification in a pocket.
- Unless you're walking on a track, don't wear headphones; you cannot hear traffic clearly.

Chapter Six

PrayerWalk Partners

Prayerwalking is just too good to keep to yourself. When I first started, I was so excited about the changes God was making in me that I began looking for partners so they could reap the same benefits. Elaine from my Sunday school class soon joined me, and I enjoyed her companionship and enthusiastic prayers. Elaine is a faith-full woman who has certainly seen the hand of God in her life. I am a rather matter-of-fact person, journalistic and to-the-point in my prayers. Elaine is a prayer warrior who passionately calls on God's power to effect miracles.

I failed Elaine as a prayer partner, however, because I had preconceived notions of how our prayerwalk should look. She prayed aloud; I felt awkward praying out loud, so I asked her if we could pray silently. I immediately sensed this request discouraged Elaine a bit. Although Elaine had to quit shortly after we started—for unrelated physical symptoms—recently I called her and asked her forgiveness for forcing my prayerwalking notions on her.

After Elaine stopped walking, I walked for more than a year alone. Instead of asking people directly if they wanted to prayerwalk with me, I placed an ad in our church bulletin. No one answered it. I think God kept me walking alone for a reason. I needed to learn to consider a companion's needs instead of demanding that she adapt to mine. When no one answers your ad for months, you should begin to wonder if your "price" is too high. These were my prayerwalking expectations: walking only at five in the morning at a certain pace for a certain time along a certain route on certain days.

I did have a prayer partner, however. For more than six years June and I have called one another nearly every day on the phone, and we often pray over the line for whatever crisis we're facing. We had also walked during the warm months. Essentially, we were walking partners and prayer partners, just not prayerwalking partners. But all those months I walked alone I assumed June didn't want to prayerwalk with me because she hadn't mentioned it. Frankly, I didn't think she was interested. Besides, June was seventy-five; surely she couldn't keep up with my pace! I was surprised when she asked if she could prayerwalk with me.

Then one day God reminded me of a story I had written years ago. After the *fourteenth* rejection slip, it occurred to me: *Duh. Maybe I ought to change it.* When I reread the article—a true, personal experience story—I realized that one scene revealed a self-righteous streak and that I needed an attitude adjustment. I adjusted it and took the scene out, and the story sold on try number fifteen.

That reminder caused me to rethink my expectations of a prayerwalking partner. So when June asked if she could prayerwalk with me twice a week, I tried to think of her needs. I asked her if I could drive to her house in the country instead of her coming into town. She thought, however, that the level, lighted Main Street would be a better course than the ups and downs of her hilly and poorly lit community. We now prayerwalk two days a week together. The walk is shorter and the pace slower than what I do when alone, but it's worth it—and good for me.

Why Enlist a Partner?

It's easy to become a lone wolf in today's busy world, but this is not biblical. We are urged in Hebrews 3:13 to "encourage one another daily, as long as it is called Today, so that none of you may be hardened by sin's deceitfulness." Part of that deceit, I think, is the idea that we can make it alone. Conversely, I have found that prayerwalking with June, or at times with another friend, strengthens my prayer vision, as well as our friendship.

Here are some reasons you may want to seek a partner:

Safety. Your community may not be safe for walking without a companion.

Accountability. It's hard to keep to an exercise discipline by yourself. Knowing your friend is waiting on the corner is a great incentive for tying on the shoes and heading out the door.

Companionship. Prayerwalking can be lonely. Some days the needs I see seem overwhelming. A partner shares this load as you can divide up the list of needs, as well as double the insight and encourage each other personally. "Two are better than one, because they have a good return for their work: If one falls down, his friend can help him up. But pity the man who falls and has no one to help him up!" (Ecclesiastes 4:9-10). When I feel down, my prayer partners pray for me—something I often forget to do.

If your husband could join you, the companionship would be that much sweeter. Because one of us needs to be home with our kids, my husband can't join me in prayerwalking (nor does he need exercise, as he spends his day hauling hay, building fences, and muscling cattle!). Even though I love prayerwalking with friends, there is something very heartening about hearing your husband pray for you.

Perspective. When you are called to any ministry, you might find yourself someday wearing self-inflicted martyr stripes. Putting all those miles on your shoes can give you an overinflated view of self-importance. I was beginning to think of Main Street as *my* prayerwalking territory. When I couldn't find a partner for such a long time, I thought, *Well, maybe it's to be my ministry alone.* Yuck! Dumb, arrogant me, again. Our Personal Trainer, Jesus, sent the disciples out in pairs: "After this the Lord appointed seventy-two others and sent them *two by two* ahead of him to every town and place where he was about to go" (Luke 10:1, emphasis mine). God likes us working together. In fact, prayer and the purification process and working together seem to be mutually dependent. The prophet Zephaniah said: "Then will I purify the lips of the peoples, that all of them may call on the name of the LORD and serve him *shoulder to shoulder*" (Zephaniah 3:9, emphasis mine). When I prayerwalk with a friend, I sense that God is purifying my thoughts and lips as I pray, as well as developing unity in ministry.

Patti says that her prayerwalks with her sister Debi and her friend Dena are "like beautiful music. Many times there are tears, many times there are confessions, many times we 'bleed' all over each other...but always we pray and God frees us from the bondage of ourselves."

Agreement in prayer. Christ has told us there is power in praying together. "Again, I tell you that if two of you on earth agree about anything you ask for, it will be done for you by my Father in heaven. For where two or three come together in my name, there am I with them" (Matthew 18:19-20). There is power in prayer when two believers agree because Christ, who sits at the right hand of the Father, becomes the third strand in that prayer. I love the assurance this brings as I pray with my friend who shares a common interest or vision.

When I intercede as my prayerwalking friend listens, our prayer partnership becomes a form of prayer accountability. It's harder for me to be selfish in prayer when someone else is listening. When I pray with my friend, I tend to center more on what God might want rather than what I might want.

Debi and her sister Patti started prayerwalking because of their compassion for teenagers. They had prayed together for years and had seen many prayer victories, including their mother's healing from cancer and Debi's teenage son's return to the Lord. Debi had participated in a yearly prayerwalk around her northern Alabama community's high school. When her church decided to plan a crusade, the leadership asked if she would head up a prayer effort.

"My heart was burdened for the kids who had nobody," she said. The women started praying that the crusade would actually be able to get into the public schools. "The kids will do anything to get out of class," she said, adding that the church arranged for crusade speakers to talk at the high school with kids who were interested.

Debi felt the need to walk around the schools while praying and convinced Patti to meet her there four days a week at 5:30 A.M. Soon Dena joined them. They feel that praying on site illuminates them about the needs at the school. They pray authoritative prayer against negative forces and have a long list of requests—for the school to be godly, for administrators and teachers, for teenagers to see the need for God.

They decided to continue even after the crusade. Although they started out as a short-term prayer project, Debi said they're "open to what God leads us to do."

She has been encouraged by an administrator who told her he felt the school's matters had been going better since the ladies' prayerwalking had begun. He also asked her to pray for him.

Tricia invited her friend Tara to join her in prayerwalking when Tara expressed an interest in growing spiritually. Tricia says that prayerwalking with Tara is more like discipleship and faith-building. When they begin at 5:30 in the morning, they first share Scripture verses or talk about what God is doing in their lives. They also discuss what they're reading in whatever book they are studying together. Then they pray—for each other and the neighbors and their needs as they walk their route.

Tara's faith has grown in just the year they have been walking together, largely because of the prayer time they have had together. Tara had a history of fertility problems, and after endless tests the doctors had told her that it would be impossible for her to get pregnant without drug treatments. She and Tricia had been praying that Tara would get pregnant. One morning Tara told Tricia that she had dreamed that she had had a baby girl. "The thing was," said Tricia, "I had dreamed about a baby girl too." A couple of weeks later Tara learned she was pregnant, *without* any drug treatments. Tara and Tricia both believe that God had healed her body, and Tara is now convinced that God does answer prayer.

Although Tricia enjoys the contemplative solitude of prayerwalking alone, she knows that God has called her to nurture Tara and loves the efficiency of meeting God, walking, and discipling her friend all at once.

So How Do You Find a Partner?

If you are drawn to the idea of having a prayerwalk partner, pray that God would show you whom to walk with. When you have clear direction, call or visit that friend and ask her directly. The burning bush didn't call Moses to lead the Israelites; God did. Jesus didn't pass a note around the Last Supper table asking if someone would stay up with him while he prayed in the Garden of Gethsemane. He *recruited* Peter, James, and John. My insecurities kept me from asking; if you don't ask someone, you won't be rejected, you see. But it's also possible that others didn't seek me out for the same reason—fear of my rejection of them.

You might consider:

- your current prayer partner or walking partner
- women who have similar interests
- women at your work

- a fellow homeschooling mom
- a family member
- women in your church small group
- a neighbor woman with a similar schedule
- someone you have met in an exercise class (Think of the money you could both save!)
- someone you would like to get to know
- someone who could mentor you in your faith or someone you could mentor

If you feel God is leading you to a specific prayerwalking partner, invite her to tea or to get ice cream or to take a walk. Explain why you want to prayerwalk and why you'd like to have a partner. Ask her if she'd be interested, and if she is, be sure you discuss what you expect in that situation. Give her time to pray about the commitment—and then you pray too.

Don't limit yourself to walking partners. A person doesn't have to be a walker to be your prayerwalking partner. I have asked a half-dozen or more ladies to pray weekly for me during their Bible study time—for my welfare and encouragement as I walk. They don't walk with me, but I am very encouraged by knowing they have already prayed for my ministry. Some of my friends who are driving to work while I walk also pray for me, as I pray for them. It's wonderful to see them wave and know prayers are being uttered in my behalf.

Things to Talk About Together as You Begin

Amos 3:3 says, "Do two walk together unless they have agreed to do so?" If you're not in agreement with your partner about your prayerwalk, it might not last long. Once you have found a partner, it's a good idea to talk through the following considerations so that there aren't misunderstandings or hurt feelings.

The need for confidentiality. You both must agree that all prayers are confidential. Gossip, even in the name of a prayer request, destroys relationships. It's important also not to judge your friend. Almost any prayer requires vulnerability, as though you were taking the bandage off a wound. Gossip or judgment is like grinding sand in the wound, causing more damage than the original sore. In contrast, a prayerwalking partner can be a salve for the soul as prayers are uttered that otherwise would not have had voice.

Your fitness levels and expectations. You may be fit enough to run track, but your partner may just be beginning a walking routine. (You may want to discuss the walking tips I give in chapter 5.) The following questions are a guide:

- How far should we walk each day?
- How fast should we walk?
- How long should we walk?
- Are there any medical considerations the other should know?

The logistics. You'll also want to agree how this will all take place, so there is a firm commitment in this prayerwalking partnership.

- Which days of the week should we walk?
- What consistent time of day could we meet?
- Where should we walk?
- How will we notify each other when we cannot prayerwalk someday?

- What weather conditions would cancel a prayerwalking date?

  Your views on prayer. How do you want to pray? Silently? Aloud? A mix? June and I chat for a bit, give praise to the Father silently, then begin our intercession aloud. We take turns. Whatever your format, you'll want to discuss beforehand how you each would be most comfortable in prayer and figure out a compromise if you differ. Chat about and work through the following questions before you head out together:

- How should our time be focused—praise, confession, intercession, listening?
- Will we pray aloud?
- Is other conversation okay? How will we limit that and stay focused on prayer?
- How will we allow our route to direct the focus of our prayers? Will we pray only for our own needs or also for those we encounter?

Double Your Insight

I wish for you all a partner for at least one of your prayerwalking days. June has brought new insight to my rounds.

"Who lives there?" she'll ask.

"Gee, I don't know," I'll say.

She'll pray, "Father, bless those folks…"

But if you can't find a prayerwalking partner, you might find companionship and safety in canine numbers, as does my friend Sue who lives on the edge of Tucson. She said that when they first moved there, they were without friends, family, or a home church.

Right across from their house, however, was a lot of open desert with a wash cutting through. Every morning at 6:30, before it got hot, she would leash up her dogs and head out to walk and pray. "It definitely wasn't the uninterrupted time we would all love to have with the Lord, but having the dogs along did keep me on my toes and help open my eyes to blessings from the Lord," she said.

"My prayers were usually lavishly peppered with comments like 'Ebony, knock it off!' and 'Dodger, stay out of the cactus!'"

She said that every once in a while she had to stop to remove cactus spines from one of the dogs. But even then, Sue said, it almost felt as if God were standing behind her, watching as she yanked each spine out with the pliers and waiting for her to resume their walk.

"Then there would be the occasional romping times, times when the dogs would just get silly and take turns chasing each other through the desert. Those are the times I would laugh and thank the Lord for blessing us with such loopy animals to bring joy to my life."

Sue said those times helped her set the tone for her entire day. It reminded her Who was in charge of all the little things that came her way. Many times the dogs would get a longer-than-usual walk because she was enjoying her prayer time so much.

With a partner—no matter what form—I think you'll find your eyesight and insight are doubled.

Part 2

Becoming a Woman of Prayer

Chapter Seven

Prayer Tips from My Personal Trainer

I was crossing a corner one morning when I remembered the gist of a passage from the Sermon on the Mount:

> And when you pray, do not be like the hypocrites, for they love
> to pray standing in the synagogues and on the street corners
> to be seen by men. I tell you the truth, they have received
> their reward in full. But when you pray, go into your room,
> close the door and pray to your Father, who is unseen. Then
> your Father, who sees what is done in secret, will reward you.
> (Matthew 6:5-7)

Was it okay that I was praying on the corners? On the streets? Out in public? Is prayerwalking okay with God?

I decided to look to Jesus to answer my questions about prayerwalking. If he were to be my mentor—my Personal Trainer for prayerwalking—then I needed to know more of what he did and said about prayer. I've never had a personal trainer, but I did have a great weightlifting teacher once. He showed me the exact form to follow in leg presses or curls—all the stations on a universal gym. I couldn't lift as much weight as he could, but I could emulate his form. Following his example kept me from injury as I pushed my body to do things it hadn't done previously. Slowly I grew in strength and endurance.

Even though we'll never carry the same weight in prayers as did the Lord who bore our sins, when he is our Personal Trainer in prayer, we can become stronger as pray-ers. So I decided to study the gospels to learn more about Christ's prayer life: where he prayed, when he prayed, what he prayed, and what he taught about prayer—directly and through parables. From my study I could gain answers to my questions.

Does It Matter If I Pray in Public?

Although he teaches us in the Sermon on the Mount to pray in a closed room, Jesus often prayed outside. "But Jesus often withdrew to lonely places and prayed" (Luke 5:16). Before he called his disciples, he "went out to a mountainside to pray, and spent the night praying to God" (Luke 6:12). After the feeding of the five thousand, "he went up on a mountainside by himself to pray" (Matthew 14:23). Before his betrayal by Judas, Christ prayed at a garden in a place called Gethsemane, outside Jerusalem's east wall, across the Kidron Valley and on a lower slope of the Mount of Olives where poorer pilgrims camped during Jewish festivals. It would be reasonable to assume that he also prayed when he fasted in the wilderness for forty days before being tempted by Satan (Matthew

4:1-11) and after John the Baptist was beheaded when Jesus "withdrew by boat privately to a solitary place" (Matthew 14:13).

I would love to hike alone to a mountaintop to walk and pray; there are literally dozens around my valley. But I don't have the time to do that. Therefore, most mornings I walk the length of Main Street and back three or four times. On summer days when I don't teach school and can take more time, I head out a county road into the valley. Once in a while I'll use the walking track at the park. I don't pray aloud unless I'm with my partner, and it's not my intent to be seen praying. People see me walking, not talking.

I view myself as a prayer pauper, someone who has nothing fancy to offer God. I leave my home each morning with a groggy head, a yawn, and seemingly nothing more to give God than myself. By the time I return, though, I have been reminded that I am made in the image of Christ. Jesus was never ostentatious when he prayed; his prayers were private. He prayed in order to spend time with the Father, not to gain others' attention and praise. I am convinced that, as long as our motive is the same, we can pray anywhere.

What Might I Pray About?

To answer this question, I studied the prayers Jesus prayed. Because he usually met with God alone, Scripture records only ten of Christ's prayers.[1] These prayers help open our eyes to how we can pray as well.

Begin with praise. Christ began the Lord's Prayer with words of praise ("hallowed be your name," Luke 11:2). In his longest recorded prayer, he calls the Father "Holy" and "Righteous" (John 17:11,25)—simple, perfect praise.

It's easy to give praise when things are going our way, but it's important also to praise God when life isn't working out. While the twelve apostles were headed off on their first mission, Jesus continued his Galilean ministry. Even though cities did not repent after seeing his miracles, he gave praise: "I praise you, Father, Lord of heaven and earth, because you have hidden these things from the wise and learned, and revealed them to little children. Yes, Father, for this was your good pleasure" (Matthew 11:25-26).

I begin my walk with, "Good morning, Lord!" Okay, yes, some mornings I'm not that perky and there may be a few groans first as my joints protest. But then I move to a time of praise: for who God is, for what he has done, for whatever will happen that day. (Chapter 8 will discuss more specifically how prayerwalking can enhance your praise time.) My praise often takes the form of Scripture or a hummed hymn or praise chorus. I don't sing aloud very often—remember, it's well below freezing most mornings I walk—and when you're walking aerobically, you can't sing. But I'm sure God knows the praises that are welling in and spilling over from my heart.

Thank God. Jesus prayed, "Father, I thank you that you have heard me" (John 11:41). God's provision for us in so many ways can inspire our thank-yous.

Offer forgiveness as needed. On the cross Christ prayed, "Father, forgive them, for they do not know what they are doing" (Luke 23:34). This is an important prayer for our lives as well. It will flush out anger, hatred, bitterness. Balanced with that, I also ask God to search my heart for the repentance that I need to do.

Lament. The psalms are full of laments, and we have one from Christ also: "*Eloi, Eloi, lama sabachthani?*" which we learn means "My God, my God, why have you forsaken me?" (Matthew 27:46). God knows when we feel alone. He knows when my heart is breaking, so why not just pray it all out? I give him my tears and hurts and questions and disappointments. (Yes, I carry tissue when I prayerwalk.)

Intercede for yourself and others. Christ prayed for himself. In the Upper Room prayer in John 17, Jesus asks the Father in the first five verses to "glorify me in your presence with the glory I had with you before the world began" (verse 5).

I often feel like weeping when I read Christ's chapter-long prayer in John 17 because it is for me. Twenty-one of the twenty-six verses were uttered on behalf of his disciples and other believers. He prayed for their protection, sanctification—growing holiness— and for their experience of joy and God's love. I was so moved and inspired by the knowledge that Christ had prayed for me in this prayer that I now pray for the future of my town. I pray not only for those who live here but also for those who will live here, the future worshipers of God.

Like Christ, you and I can pray for the protection for those driving to and working at hazardous jobs, for faith or deepened faith (a process of sanctification) for all who pass by. You or I may be the only person who really sees the needs of that mother pushing her cranky toddler, the only person who notices that the deliveryman looks especially tired, the only person who intercedes as cars fail to yield to the speeding ambulance. Ask your Personal Trainer to give you his eyes as you prayerwalk.

Ask for God's will. Both in Gethsemane and on the cross, Christ prayed for the Father's will. The Gethsemane prayer—"Yet not as I will, but as you will" (Matthew 26:39)—set up his last uttering on the cross: "Father, into your hands I commit my spirit" (Luke 23:46). In Jan Karon's Mitford novels, her main character, Father Tim, says "Yet not as I will, but as you will" is the prayer that never fails, and that is how I often pray when I don't know what God wills.[2]

When I started prayerwalking, I was petrified that my daughter Rebekah was smack in the middle of Los Angeles. Two years later, when I began writing this chapter, I was spending extra hours praying as she traveled for almost a month in Turkey, doing earthquake relief and church planting. I was not worried about her being in a country halfway around the world that is overwhelmingly Muslim and where Christians who had converted from Islam were found murdered along roadsides the month she was there. However, I was certainly concerned when I got this e-mail:

> I can't give you too many details until I get back now because of a couple incidents that happened. One of the girls on our team got a threatening e-mail telling us to stop what we're doing because it could be dangerous and that we should just go home. Also, we think that the police are following us closely here in our new location. Some guy showed up last night asking for a room, and Ryan was pretty certain he was on the police force

because he wanted to know what we were doing, when we were leaving, etc. ...

I love you, though, and keep praying because we still have some important work to finish here that we want to complete.

Instead of worrying or getting upset and ill, as I might have before, I prayed for God's will, and he gave me a peace about all of Rebekah's travels and contacts. I realized that because I had learned to give over my concerns to prayer while I walked, the way my body responded to stress had changed. My nervous stomach, neck aches, headaches, and sore jaw are only rare visitors now, rather than constant companions.

Even so, I was sure glad to get a collect phone call from Los Angeles International Airport:

"Hi, Mom, I'm home."

"You're home safe—in L.A.?" I said.

"Yup! Well, bye, Mom, I gotta go. I love you!"

Later I had to laugh: Safe in *L.A.?* No one's safe in L.A.!

Listen. Jesus not only spoke to the Father but heard from him as well. Three times God's words to his son are recorded in the Gospels for us. The first was after John baptized Christ: "And a voice came from heaven: 'You are my Son, whom I love; with you I am well pleased'" (Mark 1:11; also Matthew 3:17 and Luke 3:22). These words are then echoed after Jesus' transfiguration: "While he was still speaking, a bright cloud enveloped them, and a voice from the cloud said, 'This is my Son, whom I love; with him I am well pleased. Listen to him!'" (Matthew 17:5; also Mark 9:7 and Luke 9:35). The third time is recorded in John 12:28. Jesus prayed that his Father's name be glorified, and the response from heaven was "I have glorified it, and will glorify it again."

I often hear from God. Sometimes it's a directive: *Call Jane today.* Sometimes it's a word of affirmation, as those to Christ were: *You are my workmanship* (from Ephesians 2:10). Sometimes it's just a sense that God will cause everything to work out in my day ahead. And sometimes he gives me a little gift. When I find a coin, my friend Judy has taught me to remember, because of the inscription "In God we trust," to trust God for the very thing that has been weighing on me. Recently, while praying intensely for a teenager I'll call Chris, I found a coin every day for twelve days in a row just after praying for him. I just don't think those were coincidences; I think God was speaking to me in a very tangible way. The evidence was that in the middle of those days Chris made a recommitment to follow Christ.

How Might I Pray?

In Christ's parables and other teachings, we also learn greatly about the manner in which we can pray.

Pray simple prayers. The purpose of the Lord's Prayer was to teach us to pray simply. Jesus prefaced the prayer by telling the people listening that they should not pray as pagans do, babbling with too many words. As a former journalist and now an English teacher who appreciates succinct writing, I love that instruction. God doesn't need a whole sermon—he will get the idea from the three-point outline. Here is Christ's example of praying simply:

Our Father in heaven,

hallowed be your name,

your kingdom come,

your will be done

> on earth as it is in heaven.

Give us today our daily bread.

Forgive us our debts,

> as we also have forgiven our debtors.

And lead us not into temptation,

> but deliver us from the evil one. (Matthew 6:9-13)

God doesn't need to know the seventeen reasons why I want the children ministered to at the day-care center I pass each morning. He knows all that. It is enough to pray simply, "Father God, give the day-care workers love, patience, and sensitivity for each child they meet. Help them be the best substitute mommies they can be today." God just needs to hear from us in simple terms.

Pray with a clear conscience. Forgiveness seems to be crucial to answered prayer. Christ says that if we do not forgive others, our Father will not forgive us (Matthew 6:14-15). In a parallel teaching Jesus says we should be reconciled with our brother before making an offering (Matthew 5:23-24). If our prayerwalking praise is an offering, then we should be heading out with a clean heart. We can't pray effectively if there is a rift between another person and us.

Because I value my accessibility to God's throne, I actively pursue reconciliation in my own life. One time I had been praying for unity on my high school staff as I prayerwalked around my school, and then one day, *wham!* It hit me that I had not been supportive of one of my teaching peers. She had tried to make my life easier by relieving me of a huge responsibility, and then I said I'd do it anyway. I put a bow on a box of tissue as a peace offering and told her I was sorry I had not appreciated what she had done for me. P.S. I didn't coach the senior play that year. Whew!

Be persistent. In Luke 18 Jesus tells a parable about a widow who kept coming before a judge, pleading for justice as she faced an adversary. Even though the judge refused at first, she was doggedly persistent, and eventually the judge granted her request. Christ closed the parable with these words, "And will not God bring about justice for his chosen ones, who cry out to him day and night? Will he keep putting them off? I tell you, he will see that they get justice, and quickly" (Luke 18:7-8).

When we determine to pray with passionate persistence—with a refusal to quit despite boredom, despite discouragement, despite how things look to us—God will reward those prayers with his just and timely response.

Pray bold prayers. God wants us to be bold in our prayers. Christ said, "Ask and it will be given to you; seek and you will find; knock and the door will be opened to you. For everyone who asks receives; he who seeks finds; and to him who knocks, the door will be opened" (Luke 11:9-10). He says he won't give us a snake if we ask for a fish, or a scorpion if we ask for an egg (Luke 11:11-12). He is the giver of good gifts.

I've seen amazing answers since I have started prayerwalking, in my own life as well as others', so I know I can pray boldly to a

God who has done bold things in his name. I pray for each merchant on Main Street and for his or her spouse by name. I am convinced that I am prayerwalking by their businesses for a reason. If I know any personal needs, I pray for those specifically.

One woman has a degenerative disease that is causing her slowly to lose her sight. I hurt for her and her husband as I walk by their restaurant each day. I am praying for healing for her and for God to be glorified in that healing, resulting in their deepened relationship with God.

One man lost two employees in a car accident. Each was driving to work in the dark morning hours, and their trucks mysteriously collided on a nearby mountain road. I physically feel the heartbreak of this man as I pass his business each day and pray for comfort for all those involved.

Pray boldly. Christ says that as a father won't give a son a stone when he asks for bread, our heavenly Father will give good gifts to those who ask boldly.

Pray with faith. Jesus rebuked a demon clear out of a boy after the disciples had failed (Matthew 17:14-21). He told the disciples they failed because they had so little faith. He says that we can move mountains if we have faith even as small as a mustard seed. In Mark 11:22-26 Christ says if we believe that our prayers will be answered, they will.

Faith is belief and trust in God and loyalty to him, even when it doesn't seem logical. It's often challenged when our prayers are not answered in the way we expected. I experienced this just over a year ago with the death of my dad. At another time it hurt when my friend Jane had surgery that meant she would never bear a child. And why did my student's father kill himself? I had been praying for that family! However, I can still grow in faith through these tough prayer disappointments because I know that God is sovereign and God is good. I just see the outside of the buildings I pass as I prayerwalk; I don't know how God will ultimately work through the individuals behind those walls.

Now, I am pretty faithful. But full of faith? That's an area of growth for me. A bold request requires a bold faith. I am challenging myself in this area by reading and studying the Bible consistently. The more acquainted I become with the Creator and the God of the patriarchs, judges, kings, and prophets, and with the Lord who walked to Calvary, the greater my faith grows. When I read how the Israelites turned to foreign gods time and time again, I literally wept with the prophets. As I read all the way through the Old Testament and started reading Matthew, I began to understand God's persistent, faithful pursuit of his people. I can believe in the second coming of Christ, because my faith has been built through nearly two thousand pages of his love story. I can ask for healing, because I have read pages and pages about how Jesus healed people. I can ask that my friends' marriage be restored, because I know he abhors divorce. I can ask for protection of my family as they work and travel, because Christ asked his father for protection for his family, the disciples.

Finances always stretch my faith. I married a man who I thought would be a rich lawyer, but I ended up being hitched to a farmer (yes, he's the same guy!). Somehow we make it from month to month, but one test came up recently when my thirteen-year-old computer sighed its last byte and bit the dust. My credit card tempted me: "Use me! Use me!" It seemed logical to just go buy a new computer. How could a writer be without one? But instead I decided to see what God would do. Within days a check for $2,500 came in the mail. The Chicken Soup folks had bought a story I had written years ago for a magazine, and the magazine was sending me the royalty. This was the first I had heard about it. Honest.

If I hadn't just read about how God provided manna to the Israelites in the wilderness only as they needed it each day, I would have pulled out the plastic. Isn't that what we often do? We forge ahead with a quick plastic fix when instead we should be waiting for the manna of God to appear in our wilderness. As I'm prayer-walking, I am learning daily to depend less on the plastic whatevers of my day in expectancy of the miraculous manna. I'm not nagging my older son anymore about going to church; I'm praying with faith that God will lead him back. I'm not lashing out with sarcasm at Craig as a tactic to get my way or prove my point; my prayers for self-control are helping me bite my tongue. Oh, friend, yes, sometimes I feel like the prayer pauper as I petition God, but he is building my faith as I follow him through the pages of his Word and on the streets of my town.

My Personal Trainer can be yours, too. Don't bother to check the Yellow Pages. Trust me: He's the best.

Chapter Eight

"Great Is Thy Faithfulness"

When I took my job at the high school, I thought it'd be a great way to stay close to my oldest two kids who were then a freshman and a sophomore. However, I soon found that my being at the school mortified them. When we passed in the hall, I learned not to touch, wave at, speak to, or even smile at either of them. That lesson came quickly when I once tried to put my arm on Rebekah's shoulder as she stood at her locker. She turned around, gave me the Stare, turned back to her friends, and muttered, "It's my *mother!*" as though I were some sort of disease.

There were only two situations when they'd approach and talk to me:

Reason No. 1: When they needed money

Reason No. 2: When they wanted the car keys

On those occasions they'd mutter the few words of request and stick their hands out, looking to see if anyone was watching.

Now I know how God might have felt in the early months of my prayerwalking, as well as the rest of my life before then. I was a "gimme" pray-er. Gimme this. Gimme that. Gimme that again.

Now that my oldest kids have slipped out of the teen years, I know the joy that comes when they choose to spend time with me.

"You're not going anywhere tonight?" I asked twenty-year-old Justin one spring-break evening.

"Nope."

"Just gonna hang around home?"

"Yup." Pause. "Want to play some cards, Mom?"

Wow. Want to play some cards? Of course I did. I have learned in recent years that hanging-around time—lulls when he or she doesn't want to do anything in particular except be with me—is the most precious time I can have with my child.

Again, I think I have an idea of how God must feel when I simply choose to hang around him while I prayerwalk. I don't have any requests in mind. I just want to give him praise and thanks—and simply be in his presence.

The Forgotten Prayer

Praise is often the forgotten prayer. The writer of Psalm 100 exhorts us to "Enter his gates with thanksgiving and his courts with praise; give thanks to him and praise his name" (Psalm 100:4). I imagine myself on holy, templelike grounds as I enter into his presence each morning. That isn't hard for me to do since I live in an area that is so beautiful it can stun one's senses. Not even the streetlights can hide the deep, black starry sky. In the fall we're blessed with light shows of falling meteors—I saw a couple just this week—and I often find myself beginning my time of praise with,

> O LORD, our Lord,
>> how majestic is your name in all the earth!…
>
> When I consider your heavens,
>> the work of your fingers,
>
> the moon and the stars,
>> which you have set in place,
>
> what is man that you are mindful of him?
>> (Psalm 8:1,3-4)

Then I'll fall into a time of prayer that I call *observational praise*. I simply take in the wonder of God's creation and adore him with "you" statements:

- "You are amazing, God."
- "You create reminiscences of one creation in another."
- "You created this mountain ahead of me we call Elephant Head. In just this one big hunk of earth and stone, you remind me of a formidable, whimsical animal halfway around the world."

I look for the intricacies of trees and praise God for how the upturned branches remind me to lift up my voice and hands in adoration of him. I see that the yellowed aspen leaves skipping across the road resemble tossed gold coins and praise the Creator for a reminder to rush to him with all that I can offer. I notice the particular bend of the creek and its carved-out banks and recall how the unstoppable force of floodwaters swept through our community and made a lake of our neighborhood four times since we have lived here. In response I offer God my respect for his power to move mountain and water—and even the earth on its axis.

Praise Takes Focus

I work at my prayers of praise for two reasons. First, my praise could easily become a repeated liturgy with little thought behind it: "I praise you for this. I praise you for that." If we really "*consider* the heavens" and the rest of creation, we are giving some thought to the majesty of it all. I don't want my prayer time to be boring or just another list of tasks to check off. I should not be yawning when I come before my Creator, but alive and reverent. Second, when I am carefully and observationally praising him, I can get to know God better. When we focus on his character or his creation or his work in our life or someone else's, we become more aware of who he is and his presence in our life. We begin to see the Artist behind this earth's canvas when we spend time observing his creation.

When my husband was in the army years ago, I signed up for an art class one quiet, pre-children winter. I was surprised that when I arrived at the classroom on the army post, no one else showed up. That was fine with me, however. I was a little nervous about others seeing my work.

But five minutes into that first class I almost quit. The instructor, a slight man with receding, light brown hair, handed me some drawing paper and a couple of pencils. Then he folded a legal-sized piece of paper in half three times. Next he unfolded it and leaned it up against a wall on the table in front of me.

"Okay," he said, "draw this."

"What?" I said.

"This," he said, pointing to the piece of paper with eight fairly even sections.

"How?" I said.

"Stare at it until you see the shades of white," he said. Then he left the room.

Shades of white? I was young. I didn't know white had shades! There was white…and white…and *white!* But, I reminded myself, I was the art student, and he was the art teacher. So I stared at the paper. It *continued* to look plain ol' white to me—for nearly a half-hour of staring. Then all of a sudden the paper seemed to burst in color. Of course, there they were—all different shades of *white*. I used a *black* pencil to draw shades of white on my drawing paper. (I won't tell you what Craig thought of my "masterpiece" when I took it home!)

Prayerwalking allows me to spend time noticing the details of God's creation—patterns and colors and shapes and designs. It's as though I've been given laser eye surgery and can see the world afresh. Particularly when I'm walking in the summer, I feel God trains my eyes to see the wonder of his work. This doesn't mean that my praise will necessarily be flowery or poetic. It might only be "Wow, God! That's cool!" We don't even have to have the words to impress the Word—he knows when our hearts are bursting with awe. Praise is now a deep desire of mine because I've realized that God's design is so intricately vast, I'll never be able to see it all. The least I can do is notice the wonders immediately around me.

Lessons in Offering Praise

Psalms has helped me learn how to express my praise to God. If praise comes hard for you, you might consider memorizing sections of this praise-filled book. David provides one of my favorite psalms:

> The heavens declare the glory of God;
>> the skies proclaim the work of his hands.
> Day after day they pour forth speech;
>> night after night they display knowledge.
> There is no speech or language
>> where their voice is not heard.
> Their voice goes out into all the earth,
>> their words to the ends of the world. (19:1-4)

I imagine David spent a lot of time staring into the skies before he wrote this. Our praise may not sound like a psalm, but I bet even our sighs will be enough for God.

One recent morning a black-and-white dog began following me. You may remember that I haven't been particularly fond of the canine species. But this fellow seemed to want a friend. He followed me for one lap as I was beginning my praise. The second lap he stopped and seemed to inquire if I wanted his continued companionship. So I invited him along.

This started my thinking about how God created an animal that would actually provide human companionship in times of loneliness and delight in times of sorrow. I started thinking about all the different varieties of dogs, and I actually began praising God for his love and creativity in giving us dogs! Yes, this former dog hater is actually considering various strategies for talking my husband into getting a puppy.

Some mornings I simply focus on one of God's character traits:

that he is faithful, good, compassionate, gracious, holy, merciful, omnipotent, patient, just, or unwearied. One morning this month I noticed the faithfulness of the workers who head to the mill at 5:45. They reminded me of the faithfulness of my heavenly Father in my life and through the generations, as recorded in the Bible. Then I remembered the words to one of my favorite hymns:

> Great is Thy faithfulness, O God my Father,
> There is no shadow of turning with Thee;
> Thou changest not, Thy compassions they fail not;
> As Thou hast been Thou forever wilt be.
> Great is Thy faithfulness! Great is Thy faithfulness!
> Morning by morning new mercies I see;
> All I have needed Thy hand hath provided—
> Great is Thy faithfulness, Lord, unto me![1]

One afternoon I was prayerwalking out in the valley on a fairly gray, dreary day. I looked over the dry fields of tan stubble on the valley floor, which seemed to blend into the dry grasses of the stark, treeless mountainside along the east side of our valley. It looked like a continuous sheet of sameness. Suddenly my memory stumbled through this verse from Hebrews 13:8: "Jesus Christ is the same yesterday and today and forever." That one idea—sameness—led me to praise God for how he is the one point of stability around which all the changeable things of this universe revolve.

Have you thought of him as your Guardian or your Refresher or your Treasure? He is also your Fountain and your Potter and your Spring of Life. If I spend the rest of my life praising God, I'll never cover a hair of his greatness.[2]

Having a Thankful Heart

When I am dwelling on the faithfulness of God, I can't help but be thankful for those times when he has faithfully protected my driving teenagers or provided for our family's financial needs. We are encouraged in Psalm 95:2 to "come before him with *thanksgiving*" and in Psalm 100:4 to "enter his gates with *thanksgiving*" and to "give *thanks* to him and praise his name" (emphases mine). Paul tells us to present our requests to God "with thanksgiving" (Philippians 4:6). Thanksgiving is something we bring to God as we approach him.

Our list of thanks could easily be as long as our list of requests. I mean, how do we feel when we give our children what they would like at Christmas and then they don't thank us? That's not good manners! Doesn't God deserve our good-mannered, thankful hearts?

Prayerwalking gives me time to contemplate who God is and all that he has done for me so that my prayers of thanksgiving can be *more* than

> Thanks for my kids,
> Thanks for my car,
> Thanks for our health,
> And for stretching the checking account so far!

By dwelling on the creative goodness of God in what he has given me, I have learned to be thankful for things that I previously overlooked. One morning while prayerwalking, I noticed that our streets are laid out in the four directions—north, south, east, and west. I praised God for creating the order of our earth, with its magnetic north. Then I thought about my four children—how they are like the four directions, each so different, each so special. They then became the focus of my thanks. Some mornings I'll spend the whole time in thanks and forget about my "wish list."

Praying in Silence

C. S. Lewis wrote, "I still think the prayer without words is the best—if one can really achieve it."[3] I believe there should also be a time in our daily prayer life when we allow the wonder of God to well up so greatly within us that our only response is silent awe. The writer of Ecclesiastes tells us, there is a season for everything, even "a time to be silent and a time to speak" (3:7). Habakkuk 2:20 says, "But the LORD is in his holy temple; let all the earth be silent before him." Zechariah advises, "Be still before the LORD, all mankind, because he has roused himself from his holy dwelling" (2:13).

How do you pray silence?

Silence is the absence of sound—I shouldn't logically have to do anything to be silent. It may be easier to approach a definition of silent prayer by explaining what it is not. Silent, reverential prayer is different than listening prayer, which I'll discuss later. It's not waiting for answers, not listening for God's voice or leading. It's not an active expectation, a time when I expect to hear or get anything. It is also not a time when I can even hope that I am offering anything worthy. I'm just flat out adoring God with all that I am, with the little I have.

When my youngest, Bethany, was five, we took what we thought might be our last family vacation together before Rebekah and Justin started college. We went to Disneyland. I'm not sure what our reasoning was in emphasizing this as a *family* vacation because we ended up splitting into three groups. Bethany and I were buddies for the day, a perfect match. She was too short for the craziest rides, which I didn't want to go on anyway. The teacups and Dumbo rides were my favorites. Her highlight of the day, however, was hanging out with Minnie Mouse in a chance encounter on the paddlewheel boat. After we took a roll of film with Minnie, she wandered off to greet other passengers on the boat. But Bethany was so enamored that she kept following the famous mouse, even though she was too shy to actually say anything. "I just want to *look* at her, Mommy," she said. "I just want to *be* with her."

That's how I picture this prayer of awe—being with God, loving him with all my being, giving him everything I am, all without a word. If I were to put my feelings into words, it would make the moments less than they are. For me, awe is the best of prayerwalking. I can let all cares fly behind me as I pursue God in adoration as I walk. I let the magnitude of his love fall over me and give myself over to love of him. It is similar to but higher than the form of ecstatic love I experienced when I first fell in love with my husband. Being with Craig was enough. Words didn't have to pass between us. It was enough to experience our love together in a holy quiet.

How do I manage not to allow distractions to keep me off-centered? John 3:16 tells us, "For God so loved..." Just as Craig and I could be silent for a long time in our love for each other, I can stay focused in this silent prayer of awe by focusing on God's love for me. It's like a slow picking of the petals of a daisy with an endless supply, except this meditation is not "He loves me. He loves me not." Instead it's "He loves me. He loves me. He loves me…" I, in turn, figuratively receive those petals and love him back.

A Date with God

Prayerwalking is a date, an appointment with my Personal Trainer for becoming a woman of discipline, strength, and prayer. He meets me as I'm stepping out the door. He accepts my praise and thanks and lets me worship him in silent, reverential awe. In the allegorical Song of Songs the beloved says of her lover, "How right they are to adore you!" (1:4). In adoration I come closest to experiencing heaven here on earth. It is perhaps preparation for my heavenly life, when I will fall down and worship him forever. Saint Augustine said, "Those who look for the Lord will cry out in praise of him, because all who look for him shall find him, and when they find him they will praise him."[4] These prayers of adoration allow us to find our complete satisfaction in God alone—his love, his care, his presence. It is enough.

> Yea, Lord, we greet Thee, born this happy morning.
> Jesus, to Thee be all glory giv'n;
> Word of the Father, now in flesh appearing!
> O come, let us adore Him,
> O come, let us adore Him,
> O come, let us adore Him, Christ, the Lord![5]

Chapter Nine

Take a Walk with Me

The September Saturday evening was ending pleasantly. Joshua and Bethany were headed to bed, Rebekah was off to college, and Justin was out at a movie. I had gotten my Sunday lesson squared away, and Craig and I were looking forward to a quiet video together.

I was deciding on the movie when the phone rang. "Mrs. McHenry, do you know where your son Justin is?" I didn't recognize the formal-sounding voice.

"Yes, he's at a movie," I said. We have no movie theater in town. The nearest big city is about an hour away. He had driven there with a friend.

No, he hadn't. On the phone was a county sheriff's deputy. Justin's Jeep Cherokee was parked in front of a house outside town where kids had been partying. The deputy had found alcohol and marijuana. Several kids were in custody; Justin was gone—perhaps had run away. The deputy thought he might have headed into the woods or nearby creek area, and the deputy asked if I would call the sheriff's office if Justin turned up at home.

Shaking and nauseated, I hung up the phone, my thoughts

scattered in several directions at once. *Run away? Alcohol and drugs?* It was a cold, early fall evening, dipping below freezing. Justin had just worn a sweatshirt. He could die of exposure. I'd never seen any sign that he might be taking drugs or drinking. Maybe he had met a friend and gone to the movie. No, he *was* at a movie. He *said* he was going to a *movie*.

Craig headed out in his pickup truck and slowly traveled the streets and roads around our town. He called Justin's name until he was hoarse, returning a couple of hours later with no results. I prayed frantic, scattered prayers, pacing the house for an hour or so, picking up things out of place. *The house should be neat when the deputy comes by…if he comes by.* I expected the worst when the deputy called again sometime before midnight, but thankfully Justin had returned to the party. Testing clean, he was on his way home. I hung up the phone, hugged the several pillows on my bed, and convulsively cried.

When he walked in the door a few minutes later, Justin looked clean to us, too, and insisted he had just been playing Nintendo at the party the whole time. I wanted to believe him, but he had lied when he had told us he planned to go to a movie. "I knew you wouldn't want me to go to that party, Mom," he said later. I just wasn't sure what to believe anymore.

That was a little more than a week before I started prayerwalking. I became convinced that weekend that I had to begin putting my whole self into prayer on behalf of my family. Crying into my pillow every night did absolutely no good. Now I spend my tears on Main Street. But I thank God for allowing me to experience that desperate moment because, although my prayers while I walked were first centered exclusively on my family's needs, I quickly became aware of the needs of others. Daily I am faced with reminders that the world around me desperately needs God just as much as my family and I do.

It takes time to intercede for others in prayer before the Father, and prayerwalking allows for that time. Intercession is an essential ministry, not a last-minute, last-ditch effort of casually throwing things in God's lap. Prayerwalking is not an easy way to "take care of prayer" while you get good exercise. It is a call to spend rich time with God, carrying others' loads. The walking is only a means to make it all happen.

But the walking enriches the prayer time as it has opened my eyes to the needs of others. I no longer see only buildings as I walk through town; I see the needs of hurting people. Anything God puts in my path of vision is a subject for prayer. Our communities need our prayers and Scripture encourages this: "When right-living people bless the city, it flourishes" (Proverbs 11:11, MSG). Perhaps, as you take a walk with me and my Personal Trainer, you'll gain insight into how you might intercede for others as you prayerwalk.

Pray for Your Own Church

This morning after my prayers of praise, I turn right onto Second Street. It's Tuesday, so it's my day to focus prayers on my church. The white clapboard church with its bell tower is just a half block away. You don't have to be physically near it, but if you can prayer-walk around your church, you might pray for the leaders and pastor and their families by name, as well as folks in need. Pray for unity, vision, focus—anything that God brings to mind. You might even stop as I do today and put your hands on the building and ask God for protection from the enemy's attack, for a special blessing on the members and visitors and for great growth of faith in your community.

My prayers for my church leaders have changed me. When we pray regularly for someone, God develops a deep love and respect within us for that person. In the past I may have been frustrated with decisions made or postponed, but since I have started praying on a regular basis for these men and women, it's as though God has been whittling me as I pray. Negative, judgmental attitudes are cast aside as God sculpts my heart into one that loves and cares for our leaders.

Pray for Law Enforcement and Our Military

As I turn left on Lewis Street, ahead on the left is the sheriff's substation. As I walk, I pray for our local law enforcement officers. This reminds me to pray for our military as well. I pray that they will be safe and that they'll be a godly presence of protection wherever they are.

Pray for the Forgotten Ones

Next door to the sheriff's substation is the Senior Center, where the older people of our town are served delicious, nutritious meals and have many other needs met. These people are often a forgotten group. They need our prayers for health and emotional well-being.

Can they get to church as they'd like? Perhaps that could be a focus of your prayers—or their need for companionship or mentorship opportunities.

A mud pie's throw from the Senior Center is the day-care center. The little people of our towns need prayers that their surrogate mommies have extra patience and creativity and hugs to pass around. The oldest and youngest generations in our parts of the world need our prayers.

Pray for Public Servants

Just as I pass those two buildings, on my right are city hall, the fire department, and two county office buildings. The local, state, and national officials and public servants need our prayers. Despite public perception, they are often overburdened with balancing many roles as budgets are trimmed from the top down. I've had to do a little research to make sure I have all the right names as I pray, and you may want to do this as well. I'm sure they would appreciate your prayers that they perform all their tasks as to the Lord and that they not forget that we are still "one nation under God."

Pray for the Larger Christian Community

I turn left now on Railroad Avenue, follow and then cross the tracks, and head past the Assembly of God church. One great thing about living in a small town is the Christian community often found between the churches. Just a couple of weeks ago we enjoyed an Easter sunrise service at my church and a sumptuous breakfast afterward at the Assembly. Unity is a pillar of my prayerwalking focus. I pray that all the churches in my town would be one and that others would be drawn to Christ because of our oneness. As you walk by churches in your town, you may want to pray for unity and growth and transformation of the members and staff. Learn the names of the pastors and pray that they will meet regularly for fellowship and support. Pray for a strong sense of Christian unity in your area.

Pray for Business Owners

Now I've reached the other side of town, and I head back down Main Street. When I started prayerwalking, I soon was drawn— and I believe it was a calling—to pray for the business owners in our town. Our local newspaper, published only every two weeks, reminds us often to "shop locally." As I formerly worked as an office manager for my husband's law office, I am aware of the challenges of running a business in a small town. It truly is hard to make a living with only the occasional support of a thousand or so folks (including babies!). In my prayerwalks I became burdened for the couples who ran the businesses, and I started praying for financial success for them, for peace in their homes, and for their deepened faith in God.

After about six months of praying for these folks and the concerns in their lives, God gave me a vision. I was walking back into town that morning when I noticed the city limits sign. I believe it was God who gave me the picture of a sign that read instead: *A Place Where God Lives*. I imagined that people began to be drawn to our town because its people had been transformed by their faith in God into a people with love and peace and hope. I also imagined that this reputation had spread particularly because of those folks with enterprises on Main Street and the way they conducted their businesses. They were friendly. They were compassionate. They were ambassadors for Christ, glowing with the love of God. But they weren't the only ones. They were merely a kind of signpost or banner, because the whole community had been transformed by God. The people of my town were an authentic city on a hill, even though we're instead planted at the foot of a mountain. From that moment on I began to pray in earnest for my whole town.

If you feel God has given you a certain prayerwalking path and there are businesses along it, you may want to find out the names of the owners so you can pray for them specifically. Just stop and ask or make a phone call. In my small town there are only about fifteen businesses, and I know all the owners. Sometimes I even know of specific needs. Your newspaper may help you in that area.

Pray for the Schools

A block off Main Street's business section sits the junior high school. Yesterday I prayerwalked around the three schools in our town. I know all the names of the teachers at the high school and junior high, but I felt frustrated when I prayerwalked around the elementary school because I was forgetting some teachers' names. So one day I asked Pam, a teacher there, if she would join me on Mondays. She was delighted. It was wonderful the first time we walked because she had deep insights into the school's needs and could pray specifically. I silently prayed while we walked around her school; she did the same while we walked around mine and the junior high. We also didn't forget the continuation high school, also close by, and the school officials and school board members. You may also want to select a day for specific focus on your local schools.

Pray for Your Family

Well, I'm heading for home now. There it sits on its little rise. Shortly after our home was built almost twenty years ago, it was flooded twice in two years. After the second flood Craig had our house raised four and a half feet, with three feet of fill dirt brought in around it. People often wonder why we appear to have our own little hill in an otherwise sunken neighborhood. When I approach my house at the close of my prayerwalk, seeing it on its little hill reminds me of Christ's words: "A city on a hill cannot be hidden.… Let your light shine before men, that they may see your good deeds and praise your Father in heaven" (Matthew 5:14,16). It reminds me to pray that my family also would truly become a city on a hill. After all, we stick out, so it might as well be for the glory of God.

I also remember my family and friends when I prayerwalk. My prayers for them arise out of my relationship with them, so my prayer life can hardly be an exact model for your prayer life. That will come from your own relationships. But here are some of the things I lift up to God as I pray.

Our hopes and dreams. I used to feel my way through life as though it were a labyrinth. Remember the story of Daedalus, how he had to find his way through the labyrinth, avoiding the vicious Minotaur? I don't think God intends us to approach life as though it were a maze. Certainly we have many paths, many opportunities, but our pathway is known, even perhaps marked ahead of time with God's golden pen. Along with serious study of the Bible, I think prayer is the key to staying along that golden path.

When Rebekah and Justin were in their last year of high school, their youth group leader got the seniors from our church together with their parents. They laid out their hopes and dreams, and we all promised to pray for them as they sought God's will. I watched those young people—from families with no savings—become amazed when a full college education became possible through scholarships and grants.

It's important to tell God our hopes and dreams, always praying for God's will. This could include college—for our children or us—or technical training schools or apprenticeships. You might have a dream of learning a new language or learning to paint or sing or write. Your child might like to be an exchange student or go on a mission trip.

I've had some pretty crazy dreams for my kids. When Justin was a high school sophomore, I watched as he struggled to be accepted by someone, anyone. I prayed that God would bring him a good friend, and soon after Drew, also a redhead, began hanging around our house. They are still friends. When Justin was a junior, I knew that he had an unexpressed desire to be as tall as his dad, who is six feet one. Justin is now more than an inch taller than his dad. By the time Justin was a senior, he had put thirteen years of dedication into basketball and baseball. Every boy longs to be the hero of just one game, and so that became his mother's prayer. Shortly after that prayer, I watched with awe as Justin sank six three-point baskets in a row in the fourth quarter of the game, leading his team to an eighteen-point victory. The crowning touch was hearing the crowd yell, "Give it to Justin! Give it to Justin!" over and over again. I'll never forget those eight minutes, and I'll always be thankful that God heard my dream-prayer. So I pray for all my family's hopes and dreams, as well as my own once in a while. God is good to hear the requests, whether they're serious or not so serious.

Our need for wisdom. Some joke that when kids start driving, their parents learn the importance of prayer. Unfortunately, my daughter seemed to inherit my early driving skills. I was the first to knock down a ten-foot cyclone fence at my high school. Rebekah's driver's training teacher said she was the first student he had known in nearly thirty years of behind-the-wheel experience who tried to play chicken with a tree! Perhaps we are given teenagers to bring us closer to God; it seems to work that way.

I think we need special kinds of wisdom for the special seasons in our lives. Single people have different needs than married people. Moms of babies and toddlers have different needs than teenagers or empty nesters. I love Isaac Watts's prayer and make it my own:

> Lord, teach me all that I should know,
> In grace and wisdom may I grow;
> The more I learn to do Thy will,
> The better may I love Thee still.[1]

Do you remember how God blessed Solomon when all he asked for was wisdom? He became not only the wisest man ever known but also the richest. I believe God honors our prayers for wisdom, especially if we are also seeking it from his Word.

Our loved ones' safety. We can confidently pray for the safety of those we love because Christ prayed for protection for his disciples. "Holy Father, protect them by the power of your name—the name you gave me—so that they may be one as we are one" (John 17:11).

Our daily schedules. You'll find it helpful, I think, if you pray for your family's schedule: work activities, school tests or projects, sports games, appointments, dates, visits with friends, church activities, jobs—anything that would provide them a challenge for that particular day. I have prayed as my kids applied for scholarships and jobs and internships and missions programs. Whatever fills our day should be covered with intercession.

A desire for Christ-centered lives. It's the prayer of my heart that all in my family would have Christ as his or her center of daily thought, work, and play. I pray for Craig's growth as a Christian husband, father, coach, and farmer. On days when he is working as a lawyer, I pray that God will give him wisdom and use him in the resultant relationships.

I pray that my kids will become closer to each other and Craig and me. You can pray that your children will develop strong relationships with peers, that they'll be leaders in relationships at their schools, not followers. Pray that others will look to them in critical times of decision making—and that they'll meet that challenge with a godly stance. You might pray that your family will be good workers, worthy of their hire, and respected by those who work with them and those they serve. I pray that my kids will be respectful to their teachers and develop strong work relationships. You can pray that God will be at the very core of all your and your family's interactions with others.

I particularly love this prayer that was spread by St. Patrick:

> Christ with me,
> Christ before me,
> Christ behind me.
> Christ in me!
> Christ below me,
> Christ above me,
> Christ at my right,
> Christ at my left,
> Christ in breadth,
> Christ in length,
> Christ in height!
> Christ in the heart of everyone who thinks of me.
> Christ in the mouth of every one who speaks to me,
> Christ in every eye that sees me,
> Christ in every ear that hears me![2]

Health issues. Until my dad died, prayers for his health and comfort were a major focus. Since his death I have prayed for comfort for my four siblings and their families and for my mom. Your prayerwalk might take you past a hospital, as mine does once a week. Pray for the people there too—and for those in ambulances—both the ill and the healthcare workers.

Pray for Friends

Since I can't walk by all my friends' houses, I have organized them geographically by memory. I was always good at geography; in fact, it's my favorite Trivial Pursuit category. Praying geographically is a memory tie that helps me "travel" from one friend to another without forgetting any of them. As I walk from the east side of my town to the west, I pray for my One Heart writer friends, an e-mail prayer fellowship group—first for Anne who lives in Holland, then those who live in the East, and lastly those who live in the West, always ending with our "captain," Tricia, in Montana. In that prayerwalking time travel I have remembered my fifteen writer friends all across the country and "pond." You likewise can also pray for friends in your community, praying down the streets of your memory. You can create your own memory techniques for remembering prayers—or if you're just not good at remembering lists, you can carry one in your pocket.

Pray for Your Larger Community

It's easy to feel isolated from the world where I live, so I work at staying connected. Our family does not watch traditional television; we made the choice not to connect to cable and therefore cannot get reception to any network programming. (True confessions: We do have a ridiculously large video collection.) But we do read a good newspaper daily. As I am finishing up a typical prayerwalk session, I'll pick up the just-delivered paper and take it right to the kitchen counter; while I stretch, drink a glass of water, and take a few bites of breakfast, I pray over the news of the day.

A great resource to focus prayer for the world is *Praying for the World's 365 Most Influential People: 5 Minutes a Day to Change Your World,* edited by David and Heather Harpham Kopp and Larry Wilson. This guide takes you out of your prayer shell and into the world arena to effect change by praying for CEOs, actors, and world leaders, among others. I read this after I walk, but you could also skim the one-page daily reading before you prayerwalk, then focus your prayers on that person and area of influence.

Listen Up!

Craig and I attended a marriage-enrichment weekend at beautiful Lake Tahoe a few years ago. One speaker described a communication problem by saying, "Everyone's talking and no one's listening."

"I agree," I said, nudging Craig playfully with my elbow.

"With what?" he said. "What'd he say?"

Point made.

Just as your and my conversation wouldn't be right if I hogged all the chat space, we also want to remember to listen when we pray. After all, Jesus heard from the Father, and we have glimpses into those conversations.[3] God may remind you of a verse in the Bible or give you a sense of direction about your requests.

Speaking of direction, I often feel God turns me down new streets as I prayerwalk, and I find that he connects me with someone I might not otherwise have seen. Listening prayer is not dead space—it's servantlike acquiescence, like Mary's posture at Jesus' feet. That's a good place to rest as we prayerwalk.

A Sweet Fragrance

Prayerwalking helps make prayer a habit, your posture as you continue through your day. I don't stop praying when I reenter my home; I feel as though I'm breathing with God for the rest of my day. It's as though I've put on different glasses; I see life differently because of the time I have spent with God.

It is my hope that God is pleased with these offerings. John tells us in Revelation that the four living creatures and twenty-four elders in heaven hold golden bowls full of incense, which are the prayers of the saints (Revelation 5:8). Later he has a vision of a heavenly angel who "was given much incense to offer, with the prayers of all the saints, on the golden altar before the throne" (8:3). The incense, together with the prayers of the saints, goes up to God (verse 4).

There must be times when God could shake his head or finger at me because my prayers have been full of self. But it is the deepest desire of my heart that my intercessions be an aromatic fragrance to God—not so that I get my will but that my will has become so like his that every word I breathe and every prayer that even crosses my mind ever so fleetingly be sincerely pleasing to my Creator. I hope my prayers are a delightful fragrance and a sweet, sweet sound in his ears.

Chapter Ten

Eyes Wide Open

One morning before dawn I was prayerwalking in snow just a half-block from the heavily lighted downtown area when the lights suddenly went off. It wasn't a complete power failure; the post office lights and other businesses' lights were on. But it was enough to alarm me. I prayed against fear, but I still felt unsettled in my spirit. However, I continued walking and quickly approached the first downtown buildings.

The hardware store is a two-story brown building planted on a corner, with a squared-off, Old West–looking false front. The sidewalk passes under its roof overhang. Just as I got to it, its light also went out. I was in darkness except for the dim lights of the post office and gas station across the street. I sensed something telling me to turn around and go home. I wasn't a good judge of the difference between fear and caution and thought the enemy was attacking me. I kept going.

Just as I crossed the street, I noticed something peculiar. In the cramped parking lot next to the post office were a white Jeep and a white pickup, side-by-side with the drivers talking through opened windows. The parking lot had recently been blocked off, and no one used it because it was too hard to turn around in it. You didn't drive into the lot when another car was already there; it would be too difficult to maneuver. So I found it strange that two larger-than-average vehicles were there. *Something's not right,* I thought.

Just then I saw one man hand the other something. I immediately sensed that it was a drug deal. The one man facing me looked up and pointed me out to the other. I picked up my pace, afraid to turn around and run out of concern that they might suspect I thought something wasn't right. A block later I saw that they had left—the pickup going back in the direction I had come, the Jeep passing me and heading out of town. I breathed a sigh of relief until I saw him brake and do a U-turn at the last intersection of town. *He's coming back after me,* I thought and ran behind a corner auto parts store. He passed the building, and I thought he had kept going.

After a few minutes I ventured out, heading toward home. At the next corner, however, I noticed the car parked, in an alley, its engine running. I sought shelter at the local day-care center, which had just opened, and debated calling my husband, who would still be asleep. I decided not to pull him away from our sleeping kids. When I checked again, the car was gone, so I started for home, but immediately it drove by me again. In the next few minutes, as I started running home, it circled the blocks around me, following me down Main Street. At one point it stopped directly opposite me and the driver stared, then turned the corner right ahead of me. That gave me the minute I needed to run for home. I was able to slip into my house without his seeing me, but he continued to circle the block. A month later I learned that local law enforcement was looking for a vehicle exactly like the one I had seen that morning, in connection with a drug trafficker.

The fall I began prayerwalking I became aware that alcohol and drugs had a tremendous grip on many of our youth. As a teacher, I know when teens are spaced out at school, when they're changing peer groups for the worse, when they're dazed or asleep in class, and when their grades are slipping. We teachers walk a fine line; we can't have a kid arrested because he has bloodshot eyes, and few parents will accept any suggestion that their child may be involved with drugs. But I can pray.

I admit I wasn't quite ready for this kind of ministry when I started prayerwalking. I thought I'd spend a little time outdoors praying for my kids. The warfare took me by surprise.

I didn't know a lot of details that could help an investigation, but I knew that God had given me the gift of discernment for a reason. I also knew that prayer could change lives, so I began to pray authoritatively against alcohol and drugs on behalf of my community.

Jesus Prayed Authoritatively

Some of my prayerwalking seems more like prayerworking or prayerwarring—praying authoritatively against ungodly influences that are pervading my community, dividing my family, or trying to crush my own spirit. As you consistently prayerwalk, you may begin to discern negative influences in your neighborhood or town. Some call these strongholds. As you see patterns of evil, it is important that you respond to them with authoritative prayer.

Jesus prayed and spoke authoritatively on numerous occasions when forces of nature were out of control or evil spirits needed to be thrown out.

- When Jesus was approached by a demon-possessed man on the east side of the Sea of Galilee, he asked the man, "'What is your name?' 'My name is Legion,' he replied, 'for we are many.'... The demons begged Jesus, 'Send us among the pigs; allow us to go into them.' He gave them permission, and the evil spirits came out and went into the pigs'" (Mark 5:9,12-13).

- On one occasion the disciples were unsuccessful at healing a child with long-term demonic possession. Jesus spoke to the spirit: "You deaf and mute spirit,...I command you, come out of him and never enter him again" (Mark 9:25).

- In Capernaum a man possessed with a demon accosted Jesus: "Ha! What do you want with us, Jesus of Nazareth? Have you come to destroy us?" Jesus tells the demon, "Be quiet!" and "Come out of him!" And it does (Luke 4:33-35).

- He even directly spoke to the wind and the waves, rebuking them and calming them (Matthew 8:26).

Christ gives believers this same authority. When the seventy-two reported back to Jesus after going out in his name, they reported, "Lord, even the demons submit to us in your name" (Luke 10:17).

A Word of Caution

In *Prayer: Finding the Heart's True Home,* Richard Foster advises that the Christian exercise prudence here. "We must never become so enamored by the spiritual world that we think every jot and tittle of life is caused by supernatural activity, nor should we be so taken in by the naturalistic assumptions of modern society that we fail to see the markings of the transcendent."[1] Not everything in life is a battle with spirits. That wrong belief, after all, was why some of our Puritan forefathers burned to death so-called witches, who actually may have instead been just a little different from the Puritan mainstream. It's possible to turn a prayer session of any kind into a focus on Satan rather than God, to spend more time focused on worries and prayers over the Destroyer's threats rather than giving praise to the Creator.

A teacher hears a sizable number of excuses over a school year. "My dog ate my book." (Actually, her Fido did eat her book—half of it!) "My dad took the wrong car, and my homework was in it." "My paper is in my locker, but there's a dead mouse in there, and it stinks." "My cat sprayed on it." You name it, I've heard it. Students will be at their most creative when they need someone or something else to blame. We adults can be the same way. We may creatively look for a scapegoat for our sin—even Satan—when we aren't willing to 'fess up that it was our humanness that created the mess instead. Satan can take advantage of our fallen nature, but certainly this doesn't happen to us believers without our help. It's appropriate, then, as we consider the influence of the enemy, that we also acknowledge and repent of our sin.

Put on Your Armor

But evil does have its influence in our individual lives and in the corporate community. Since we know there is an evil spirit world, we shouldn't stick our heads in the sand and pretend there isn't. We can instead approach this prayer work professionally, ready and confident that God was, is, and will be the Victor.

We are told in Paul's letter to the Ephesians to put on our "full armor" (Ephesians 6:11), but what does this really mean? Spiritual warfare does not begin when you step outside your front door. When my husband served in the army years ago, he couldn't merely put on the fatigues and expect to be ready for the enemy; he had to go through basic training—months of strenuous physical challenges and classroom instruction—before he could begin his assignment. And it didn't end there. There was always morning PT (physical training)—running miles in combat boots. (Just for the record, he preferred volleyball and basketball.)

Similarly, I can't just put on my tennies and be ready for anything prayer-wise as I walk. Prayer is just one discipline. Ephesians 6 instructs me to put on and stand in truth and the Word of God, righteousness, the gospel, faith, and salvation. I think this is a two-step process. I study the Bible diligently and then live it out all day long. What does "diligently" imply? I think I put on the "belt of truth" when I read the Bible each night. I read several chapters, using a guide that helps me read the Word chronologically. Depending on my level of energy and the level of household noise, it may take twenty minutes or an hour to study, take notes, and read cross references or notes.

Oh, boy, you say, *sounds like another commitment to me.* If I were in the army, I'd respond, "Ma'am, yes, ma'am!" Just as Craig jogged his PT miles every day to stay in shape for future physical challenges, I want to study the Bible methodically and daily to be ready for spiritual challenges. Just as Jesus quoted Scripture when Satan tempted him in the wilderness (Matthew 4:1-11), the Word of God and its truth can help me meet the challenges of my day. I'll know the Word only by studying it.

The other protection for us is salvation, faith, righteousness, and the gospel of peace. When I respond with a grateful heart to the gift of salvation that God has given me and speak openly about my faith, I feel I further the gospel of peace. When I obediently live out my faith, I am choosing righteousness and am less vulnerable than if I were to make wrong decisions. Daily I make choices that allow God to transform me.

Warfare is most effective if I wake up with this attitude: *Change me, Lord. Sanctify me. Make me holy.* I can't pray for an hour in the morning and assume the battle is over. The battle is being waged everywhere: in my home as I function as mom and wife, in my teaching job (since I teach teenagers, that's a given, huh?), in my church, and in every contact I have all day long. God can use more of me more of the time when I have a sincere desire that I will become more like Christ. God can use anyone—he even used a donkey with Balaam—but it just seems more likely that he'll use us when we are covered with his attitude and filled with his spirit.

To God Be the Glory

From the gospel accounts I have concluded that these authoritative prayers need not be verbose. Typically I say aloud, "As a believer in the Lord Most High, I speak to the spirits of alcohol and drugs and command that you break your hold on our community. I tell you to go to the place reserved for you in the name of Jesus Christ, who conquered death and now lives with the Eternal God."

I'll then pray for God's Spirit to touch the hearts of those who have been afflicted with substance abuse in our town and ask that God do a mighty work to make our community that city on a hill.

Although I believe that prayer is the more important work, I also provide activities through our school for drug-free activities for our youth. I have gotten funding through county sources for trips for our kids and for events such as our Shakespeare Day, when we bring in Oregon Shakespeare Festival actors. I want to help provide other choices for teens being tempted with illegal substances.

Shortly after I began praying against alcohol and drugs in our schools and community at large, local law-enforcement officers started making regular drug sweeps through our school with trained dogs. A short time after that there were arrests of drug dealers in our community, and then a methamphetamine laboratory was broken up in a nearby community, followed by several arrests.

I don't imagine our community is drug-free, but I don't sense the oppression I had previously. Could my very plain prayers have effected these changes? No. God exposes lies and evil. God breaks up darkness. Only God changes lives in such dramatic ways. I say, "To God be the glory, great things he hath done." He is the Victor.

I merely put on my shoes, hat, and coat in the morning and spend an hour in prayer.

Spiritual Mapping

If the idea of doing spiritual warfare tugs at your soul but you don't have any idea what strongholds may exist in your community, you may want to seek out or start a churchwide or community-wide effort to conduct spiritual mapping.

This is an organized, three-pronged effort. Some people will dig into your city's history to learn of past traumas, sins, patterns of weakness, and natural disasters, as well as the history of Christian churches and other religions. Others will do physical research about how the city's buildings and street layout came to exist, noting these developments on maps. A third group will focus on spiritual research—digging into the health of Christian churches and other religious or quasi-religious facilities or organizations over the city's history. When the research is finished, a citywide team of churches will begin to pray for the dissolution of strongholds and for the awakening of a desire for only the true God.

This is a very simplistic explanation of a very involved process. If you're interested in using your prayerwalk ministry as a vehicle for this type of prayer, I'd recommend that you read C. Peter Wagner's *Breaking Strongholds in Your City.* There are also numerous sites on the Internet that could guide you into developing a prayerwalk ministry that focuses on a spiritual-mapping ministry or on neighborhood evangelism. The sites are easily found, using "prayerwalking" in your search.

Personal Spiritual Warfare

You may also experience some personal warfare, perhaps even an intangible resistance to your prayerwalking. The enemy certainly does not want God's believers to spend more time in prayer. That would mean godly change was ahead. I can just about guarantee that you'll face some spiritual struggle as you choose to spend more time with God. The enemy simply doesn't want that.

This was true for me. Certainly I faced nearly daily struggles with my alarm clock, but I didn't really consider that from the enemy. That was my phlegmatic flesh. I did have continual struggles with pain though. Remember, I began this at the end of my forties. I am not decrepit, but I'm also far from twenty-something. (I did, however, recently win a game of Knockout against a star basketball player, as well as place nine years younger than my real age in a health survey. To God be the glory in those victories as well.) When I started prayerwalking, however, I experienced a lot of leg and joint pain. My hips hurt somewhat while I walked, but the real killer was when I was trying to fall asleep at night. The pain in my hip socket area seemed controllable only with pain medication.

I also had shin splints. This is a condition involving pain in the front and sides of the lower leg that occurs or worsens during exercise. It is a common problem with runners. Shin splints can be caused by pressure from exercise or from inflammation of a tendon, muscle, or outer layer of a bone. In most cases they'll go away with a week or two of rest, but I was stubborn: I wanted to keep prayerwalking. It got so I was stretching my shins, during and after a walk and throughout the day, pulling the toe area up toward me. Whenever I thought about it, I also did little leg lifts while I sat.

I experienced the worst of this pain while walking one springtime morning in the country neighborhood near my parents' home in rural Sacramento. My dad had passed away just a few days before, and I was staying with Mom, helping her get the memorial service and other arrangements in place. It was a tough time, as my dad had been the world to me. He had been my matter-of-fact encourager; when he told me I could do something, I believed it, because when he stated something, it was so. Even in the last stages of Lou Gehrig's disease, he had a smile, a joke, and a kind word for everyone. It was hard to get out of bed that week and face the emptiness of my parents' large home. I had let prayerwalking slip for a few days and could feel the weight of the world clouding my vision once again.

So I put on my sweats and walking shoes and told Mom I would be back in an hour. The pain attacked my shins even as I headed down the driveway. I stopped and stretched. It subsided a bit, then came back again, so I stretched some more. This continued for two miles, as I hobbled to the halfway corner, where I'd turn back to head home. It was hurting so badly that tears were falling. *I'm not going to make it home,* I thought. I stopped and stretched and rubbed my shins and started looking around, trying to figure out which home to approach to use a telephone. I wasn't known in this neighborhood, so I felt uneasy about asking a stranger to let a stranger (me) use the phone. Any pressure now on my legs produced such a sharp pain that it felt as though something were broken in my right shin. It hurt that badly.

I walked to a tree that shaded the corner and leaned against it to take the pressure off my legs. *Perhaps someone I know will drive by, maybe someone from the family on the way to the house.* Much of that walk so far had been a prayer that God would take away the pain, so I felt confused about why it was continuing. Why wouldn't he take it away so I could get on with his prayer business?

As I was pondering this, the words came to me: *Pray against it.* I immediately thought of Paul's words, "I can do everything through him who gives me strength" (Philippians 4:13). With just a few moments' hesitation, I literally prayed authoritative prayer aloud against the pain in my legs. As I stood straight up, it was clear: The pain was gone. I walked a few steps, even jogged a few paces, which always made my shins ache. The pain was completely gone. I have not experienced it since then.

It had never occurred to me that pain could be a force the enemy could use to stop my prayerwalking ministry. My, but he's creative—using relationships and situations and all kinds of ways to hurt us, sometimes literally. John Dawson writes in *Taking Our Cities for God* that Satan has only two weapons, accusation and deception. In my case, the deception was that I thought I was experiencing pain over which I had no control. Once God directed me to pray, affirming that I could do all things through Christ's strength, the deception was no longer possible. I was believing in God's strength, not my weakness. The deception was over, and God became the Victor.

Prayer Targets

Prayerwalking can enhance your awareness of areas in your community that need the prayer of authority. Some of those situations could be

- dependence as a community on drugs, alcohol, and tobacco
- gang activity, harassment, and violence
- criminal activity and violence
- profanity
- pornography
- graffiti, trash, and vandalism
- hate crimes, prejudice, and intolerance
- rape and sexual abuse
- materialism
- divorce and disintegration of families
- criminal behavior of children and others in schools
- sexually active teenagers
- abortion
- AIDS and other diseases transmitted through sexual contact
- neighborhood and community blight
- suicide
- poverty and indifference to poverty
- high instance of welfare dependence
- negativity and an independent spirit—lack of respect for heritage, rules, authority
- disrespect for schools, administrators, and teachers
- homelessness

- disrespect for churches, pastors, believers, and the Sabbath
- disregard for traffic laws and others' safety
- gossip
- lack of neighborhood or community connectedness or involvement
- disconnection between generations

How Will You Know How You're to Pray?

I believe there will be clear indicators.

You will see problems and be moved emotionally. As you prayer-walk, you may see city blight or hear neighbors argue or walk past an abortion clinic. It may be your call to pray for God to intervene. One prayerwalker, Maxine, noticed that there were pockets of blight along her route. One man in the neighborhood was collecting vehicles; cars in every pastel color, it seemed, as well as a school bus, lined his yard. She had become so frustrated that she considered calling city officials about citing the man, but she was wary of making enemies.

She was embarrassed, really, when she decided to pray for him and about the problem instead. Why hadn't she thought of that first? Within a month she heard the man was moving, and within two months the vehicles were gone. She now continues to pray against blight.

If the problem is a community-wide problem, you will begin to see it repeated. One aspect of my community that disturbs me is a sense of independence. It's not so much an "I don't need you" attitude as an "I want to be my own boss" attitude. I believe this may have grown out of the Gold Rush days, when men were only out for themselves and their own financial gain. Families were left behind. Rivers were dug up. Communities were deserted when the gold panned out. I don't think it's necessarily healthy for a community when each resident thinks it's all right to do his own thing. I have seen a lot of evidence of this attitude: hirings that have not followed procedure, coaches who use tobacco on school grounds, homeowners who ignore codes in the building process, teenagers who throw parties the night after their parents leave town. I have to catch myself when tempted to disregard traffic laws or procedures at school. That's a sense of independence—thinking I am somehow above the law that has been put into place for my good. As you prayerwalk, you may see a similar negative pattern in your community. Pray against it.

If it is a community problem, you may find signs of it within your own church. I believe pornography is a nationwide problem. Parents find their kids involved with it on computers at home and homes receive it in the mail, unsolicited. I had seen little signs of it here and there in our community but knew it was an area for committed prayer when a leader in our church said he was having problems overcoming his addiction to pornography. If men and women in your church are struggling with forms of addiction or with gossip or with profanity, begin praying against it on behalf of your whole community.

The issue simply won't leave you alone. One prayer I never prayed still haunts me. Ten years ago when I started teaching, the son of very good friends killed himself when he was a sophomore. I have prayed regularly since then for the family, but it never occurred to me to pray against suicide. Four years ago another youth, also from our church, killed himself when he was in the fifth grade. These were gifted young people, both now lost to us. They have been the only teenage suicides in our very small community in those ten years—both from our church family. Oh, I wish I had known to pray against that spirit of suicide.

As those boys' suicides still haunt me, what confronts you as you prayerwalk will be your billboard, your sign that your prayers are needed. The physical reminder I see on one of my walking routes is the Little League dugout where one of those young men took his life. It still tugs at my heart over ten years later; the whole incident won't leave me alone. In response I pray aloud against suicide on behalf of my students.

I carry this passion into my classroom as well. I preach an awful lot against suicide, especially after I teach *Romeo and Juliet* to my freshmen. I even sing them a song, "You're Not Alone," originally recorded by Amy Grant. No, I'm not prayerwalking around the room when I do it, but I'm still in an attitude of prayer.

You'll find that you don't take the armor off when you step back into your home or get into your car for work or help your child with homework that night. The armor, I believe, becomes forged even more tightly, so that discernment comes more quickly, prayer becomes more natural, and strength through Christ is the result.

You're Not Alone

This arena of prayer may be completely new to you. Perhaps you were like me; you just thought you'd pray for your family. God may be calling you to use your prayerwalk as a time to praise him or to pray for your friends and coworkers or your husband and kids. Always, always, always do what you know God is calling you to do. You may find, however, that as you follow God's leading, you will begin to see needs in your community. Those needs may begin to burden your heart, especially as you see patterns and alarming evidence of them in your own church family or perhaps even in your immediate family. When these burdens won't leave you alone, it will be a natural step to ask God for discernment about how to pray. And then you will. I know you will. Please write to me and tell me you are so I can pray as well. Armored and bound together, we will stand and see what God will do. To God be the glory, great things he will do.

Chapter Eleven

A Sacrifice of Tears

It's not unusual for me to stop in the middle of my first-period class and wipe my glasses, and it's not unusual for them to need wiping because they're tear spotted as a result of my morning's prayerwalk. I can't pass by the home of a friend's mother who is dying and not shed a few tears. I can't pray for my children and husband and their heartbreaks and not break down myself.

Tears are natural when we care. Jesus wept when he approached Jerusalem: He knew that the people would not accept him as the source of true peace (Luke 19:41-44). Prayer is often a deeply emotional experience and may lead to tears: tears of intercession, tears of remorse, tears of joy, and tears of growing pains.

Tears of Intercession

When I began prayerwalking, I didn't realize that it would be a work of ministry. I knew that some people feel called to pray as a ministry, but I didn't, and so I never thought of my prayerwalking in that way. If you remember, I began prayerwalking so that I could check off "Pray" on my daily to-do list while getting some good exercise. I felt I would then be better equipped for my other areas of ministry. Wrong. I soon found that praying is hard work. In fact, Oswald Chambers wrote that prayer does not equip us for the greater works but is in fact the greater work. Prayer is the greater ministry. As an intercessor I open up my heart a lot. I feel as though I'm a 911 operator, looking and listening for others' needs and calling out to the Healer on their behalf.

In that role I take on others' pain. I would never presume to think that my prayers could lessen someone else's physical pain. I only pray; God does the work. The thing is, the pain is good. It reminds me to keep approaching God about my friends' needs. Even as I write today, I am torn. I have so many who need intercession in their behalf. My family still hurts as we all approach the one-year anniversary of my dad's death. My church is beginning a search for a new pastor, and my pastor friend of sixteen years, David, is seeking a new position. Sue is in the hospital recovering from major surgery. Jan just lost her mother after a long, difficult illness. Several friends have sons in rebellion—two talked recently of suicide. The list seems endless some days, and I weep for these people. I take on their heartaches when I pray, and my chest literally hurts.

But praying for others is more than a ministry, a service to be performed. My farmer husband Craig is also an attorney who worked for many years in a full-time, solo practice in a nearby small town. He now practices law on a limited basis; he's mostly occupied with his hay farming and beef cattle. But I know intimately what it is like to advocate for others' needs through the courts because I was his only office help for many of those earlier years. He would have lengthy meetings with clients when they would lay down their paperwork and their concerns and then leave with the expectation that Craig could fix it all. Many times this would require a petition of the court—or literally dozens of motions or other pleadings. In some cases he would make several appearances in court on his client's behalf, presenting her position and advocating for her. This was his job as a professional advocate—persistently interceding until his client received her land or bequest or custody of her child. He is a strong advocate.

As women we will find it hard to escape the emotional ties as we intercede, and perhaps we're not meant to. I certainly can't. But we need to keep in mind that, if intercession is going to be a life's pursuit or ministry or call, we must be professionals. A professional, says Webster's, is one who engages in "a calling requiring specialized knowledge and often long and intensive academic preparation."[1] As intercessors we must learn as much as we can about the Judge and his Word, so we know how to pray. Yes, it's useful to read books about prayer (I'm glad you're reading mine!), but it's more important to pray, pray, pray.

We need to be as bothersome in our prayers as a good attorney or the persistent widow in Luke 18. Just as a lawyer fills out all the paperwork and files endless motions on his client's behalf, we must petition the Father over and over. Like the widow, we must bother the Judge with our requests. My friend Dan, who also prayerwalks, calls this the picket-fence approach. His aunt told him that each prayer is another picket pounded into the ground around an individual, especially prayers that others will come to a new faith in God. Eventually the person is hemmed in completely by the picket fence of prayer, with nowhere to go except up to the Father. It's our job as intercessors to pound in those sturdy pickets, day after day after day. As the judge in Luke 18 was almost worn out by the widow's requests, the presence of the Holy Spirit as we pray for others will wear out resistance in others' lives so that God can work.

A word of warning: Persistence can be boring! Sometimes it feels as if I am playing the same cassette tape for the Lord every day. Sometimes a stray dog is more interesting than my petitions. *Is God even listening?* I wonder. Persistence is nearly a lost quality in our new millennium world of marrying a millionaire or winning a million instantly on television. But when I pray over the long haul, a sense of calling to pray takes over: I begin to care for and love those for whom I pray, and that love takes over and keeps me going. As the repetitions of weightlifting develop muscles, persisting in our prayers develops strength of faith—knowing that God will work.

In our persistence, we can even reason with God. Abraham negotiated an agreement with God to save wicked Sodom from God's wrath if fifty—then forty-five, then forty, then thirty, then twenty—and eventually if just ten righteous people could be found (Genesis 18:16-33). Apparently Abraham's pleadings changed God's intent. So did Moses' words. When the Israelites built a golden calf, Moses talked God out of wiping them out (Exodus 32:9-14). Good lawyers reason with the judge and the jury.

All of this may not even seem reasonable. Reasoning with God? I mean, I am only the created; God is the Creator. He's the King; I'm just the subject. *Intercession*—in the Greek, *enteuxis*, a petition—is the technical term used for approaching a king. Now, I've never met a king. In fact, the closest I've come to meeting a head of state was attending the inaugural ball for California's governor, George Deukmejian, some years ago when my husband was a county supervisor. When you're at the governor's party, you do things the way he'd like them done. You don't eat food unless invited; you don't venture into certain areas of the ballroom unless you are so privileged; and you don't sit in chairs that are not designated for you. In fact, it's rather funny now that I remember the evening. Craig and I never even found a chair to sit on the whole night; we just made laps around the room—I in an old bridesmaid's dress and he in his rented tux. We were just content with being invited to this party at all and with having a closeup look at the "king." We made a rather handsome couple, actually, and no one knew that we had parked our "pumpkin," a very old Chevy that badly needed a paint job, several blocks away.

The point is that I think we need to show the same respect for the Lord of the universe as we intercede for others. This life of "ours" is, in actuality, God's party. He has provided the ballroom, the food, and the purpose for the whole thing—that he be worshiped and glorified. The party isn't for me. I don't get to blow the candles out and get my wish. The only posture I should make, then, in approaching God is to ask according to God's will (1 John 5:14). It's my job to get in line with his will—even in my prayers—and then persist until God's redemptive hand moves the mountain in my friend's life.

Tears of Remorse

But prayerwalking is not only a time of intercession. The more I commune with God, the more clearly I see myself, and some of my tears are ones of remorse. Meeting God daily as I prayerwalk puts into perspective who I am. Many days I don't like what I see in the mirror of prayer. I am by nature analytical. In the past much of the focus of my analysis, however, was on the situation and others, not myself; the consequence of this posture was that I would place blame on others rather than on my own shoulders.

As I have been writing this book, I have been living through some of the greatest challenges I have faced in my near thirty years of this Christian walk. In the past I have enjoyed rewarding personal relationships, but during this school year I have received continual criticism. Comments from parents have included: "Your standards are too high." "You favor some students over others." "You are a terrible teacher." Whew! You don't know how many tears I've shed over those words and how they keep echoing in my head and heart.

In the past when I've received criticism, I would run to my Father with my hurts, as a little child would when she is bruised. I'd cry my Shirley Temple tears and pout and demand that Daddy make the bad thing go away. That had been my approach before I began prayerwalking—simply rushing into the ballroom and making my demands. In the real-world parent conferences I'd present my evidence, showing that the student was in fact negligent. When the parent then backed away from accusing me, I'd self-righteously pat myself on my back and move on.

But this year has been different. That's because with each new complaint, you see, I couldn't use the Shirley Temple approach of prayer anymore. I had grown up into a new relationship with my Father. I wasn't a little girl of faith. I no longer feel as though I can ask my Father to make the bad thing go away. Even though I may still feel I've been falsely accused, I now know that when others are critical of me, I need to look more deeply into the mirror. When I did that this year, I saw a reflection of my own pride and anger and an unhealthy sense of self-righteousness. None of that was very pretty, and I began to ask questions. Could I change my teaching methods to make the material sink in better? Could I communicate better with parents? Could I restructure my grading procedure to be as objective as possible? I decided I could, and with the help of several continuing education classes, I am making some changes. Even when change is painful—and involves tears of remorse—I will continue to pray to become more like Christ.

Tears of Joy

When I prayerwalk, I feel as though God is filling me with more of himself. I am more conscious throughout the rest of my day of the presence of his Spirit over me, in me, through me. I see this as filling the reservoir. In California the only way most of our larger communities survive is through our system of reservoirs. The spring runoff from the snow in the mountains fills dozens of reservoirs at the mountains' edges. The water, carefully managed, is then rationed to farmers in the Central Valley and to cities. In a drought year, believe me, everyone gets nervous. But in recent years there has been plenty, and in flood years sometimes the water spills over.

I see my prayerwalking as an opportunity for God to fill me. Every weekday I breathe in more of him and am filled, sometimes even overflowing—as on those days when my son catches me singing over peanut butter sandwiches. In each stressful situation I can draw from that reservoir of life. Believe me, if I miss a couple days of prayerwalking and then wham into a wall at work or at home, I can tell a difference. I'm just not as prepared without prayer.

As I experience more of God, I am sometimes moved to tears of pure joy. I found the best metaphor to express this in a little book by Henri Nouwen, *With Open Hands*.[2] That's exactly how we enter prayerwalking—with open hands, open eyes, open heart, open mind, open spirit. "Open! Open! Open!" the Mervyn's commercial used to say. It's as though I'm saying, "Everything I can possibly offer to you, Father, is yours. Use me. Do with me what you will." I sense this gives God pleasure. In fact, some days I sense that the only reason I'm walking is to be with him. No petitions. No confessions. No anxiety to dump. Sometimes we just enjoy each other's company.

Many days I'm walking alone, without a human partner, but that's okay because my Personal Trainer's walk on earth must have been lonely many times. Christ's prayerwalk took him down a lonely, rough road to the Calvary cross. At Gethsemane he asked Peter, James, and John to watch over him while he prayed (Matthew 26:36-38). The presence of his friends must have been a comfort—even as sleepily undependable as they were. This slice of Christ's life shows me that as he desired the companionship of his disciples on earth, I can know that my Lord desires my companionship today.

Some days it's as though my entire prayerwalk is only a prayer of "Here I am, Lord." In Ezekiel 22:30 the Lord said that he looked for a man who would build up the wall and stand for God in the gap on behalf of the land, so that he would not have to destroy it. He found none. If God only needs one person to stand in the gap and to pray for my community, I want to be that one person. I want to walk over the streets of my town and claim them for God. I'm willing to say to the enemy that he will not win. I'm willing to pray for the businesses and schools and local institutions, that God would be glorified through them all.

Tears of Suffering

This determination to follow God's call to pray may mean I'm misunderstood. Just about anyone whose life I touch in some way has an idea of what I should and shouldn't do with my time. But prayer is work, and the work is hard. When you're trying to be about God's business, the enemy will do what he can to keep you from it or discredit you in some way. It's possible that some tears may come as a result of humiliation; others—even loved ones— may find your prayerwalking somewhat silly at best. Humiliation, however, brings us closer to identification in the suffering Christ experienced on the cross—and that's another step forward in the sanctification process.

But even when we're feeling weak and alone on our walk, we're not alone in our prayers. Have you been to a high school football game recently? Remember the cheerleaders? The football players are running themselves weary all over the field. They don't even know how to ask for support. The cheerleaders watch and yell on the team's behalf. Well, we have a cheerleader too: The Spirit helps us in our weakness. "We do not know what we ought to pray for, but the Spirit himself intercedes for us with groans that words cannot express. And he who searches our hearts knows the mind of the Spirit, because the Spirit intercedes for the saints in accordance with God's will" (Romans 8:26-27). Even when we don't know how to pray, the Spirit is searching our hearts and interceding for us in alliance with God's will. This concept amazes me. I may not know how to frame what I want in words. In fact, I may not even know what I want! But this doesn't stop the Spirit, who researches the deepest parts of my heart and soul and then puts what he finds into petitions that God will accept.

Another advocate is the Son. Christ is at the right hand of God, interceding for us (Romans 8:34). In fact, Christ "always lives to intercede" for those who are saved (Hebrews 7:25). How can I lose as an intercessor? I've got two huge advantages: The Spirit can intercede on my behalf in a form that is acceptable to God, and the Son of God is at the Father's right hand sticking in a good word for me. The third piece of good news, prayerwalker, is that the Father is on our side too. Paul wrote that "from the beginning God chose you" (2 Thessalonians 2:13). Because God chose me, I can have hope, even through my tears, that he will grace my intercessions with favor.

On the Potter's Wheel

The beautiful paradox of prayerwalking tears is that the more you leave behind, the more of God you take with you. Although I am emotional, I am not by nature compassionate. You can ask my kids. When they get the stomach flu in the middle of the night, I don't say, "Oh, you poor thing!" but instead, "Why didn't you make it to the bathroom?" So I just have to give God credit for my changed eyesight. When you spend more time with someone, you begin to learn of their history and understand their joys and sorrows. Because of prayerwalking, I believe God has been gifting me with glimpses of his pain, and some of this has come through study of his Word. In past years I only sort of survived reading through the four hundred pages or so of the prophets. But the first year I was prayerwalking, those books of the Bible completely came alive for me. I began to see God's pain on every page. The following passage is when I was hit with a block of wood of sorts. God is speaking of mankind:

> He cut down cedars,
>> or perhaps took a cypress or oak.
> He let it grow among the trees of the forest,
>> or planted a pine, and the rain made it grow.
> It is man's fuel for burning;
>> some of it he takes and warms himself,
>> he kindles a fire and bakes bread.
> But he also fashions a god and worships it;
>> he makes an idol and bows down to it....
> He prays to it and says,
>> "Save me; you are my god." (Isaiah 44:14-15,17)

Human beings take some of the wood and use it for fuel for warmth and baking. With the remnant we fashion an idol for worship. We worship the created thing, not the Creator. Can you imagine never giving credit to Michelangelo or Beethoven or Shakespeare, virtually stripping their signature away? How much greater is the pain and injustice, then, when we fail to give the Creator of the universe our honor and worship? My prayerwalking tears are therefore often on his behalf, as I notice the V formation of geese or the first glimpse of the sun peering over the mountain or the sweet smell of lilac…and think about all who never give God even a simple nod for those great pleasures he has given us.

You see, God has stolen my heart. He is spinning it on his potter's wheel. Just as the potter uses water in the fashioning of the jar and just as the water splashes all over the place, so God uses my prayerwalking tears to fashion me into something much better than a lump of clay. My sacrifice of tears is good. Yours will be too.

Chapter Twelve

Faces of Answered Prayer

As I write, I sit surrounded by the faces of answered prayers or the faces of prayers in process. The doors that enclose my armoire-style desk are filled with photos of those for whom I pray. (Before you drool over how you picture my fancy desk, please know that I think "armoire" is a fancy name for a desk that can disguise a multitude of messes in a second.) I want you to meet some folks who have affected me during my prayerwalking experience.

The Preacher

I have a postcard of my town that features the lumber mill as seen from a nearby hillside. Inside the mill are a lot of dangerous machinery and a couple hundred folks who need to meet God. There is a growing number of women and men of the faith as well, and earlier I recounted how I began praying for the mill and its employees when I started noticing the cars busying back and forth on the highway at the shift change. The mill and its folks have become my prayerwalking family—whether they know it or not.

Victor is one of the mill clan, and he knows I pray for them. We wave at each other as he drives past me on his way to work, and later in the day I sometimes drive by him as he jogs along the roadside. His Mexican-American heritage may have seasoned some of his passion for life, whether he is competing in an alumni basketball game or watching his three boys play football.

It's hard to imagine Victor not enjoying anything he does, but he used to hate going to work. Now, however, he says the whole atmosphere at the mill has changed, with four specific results. The first is that the focus on "production first" has changed to "safety first." "Shortly after you started praying," Vic says, "the management started a safety program. While people weren't into it at first, now they are. We must read and sign a mill safety procedure and attend safety meetings every other Friday."

The second is a decrease in the use of alcohol and drugs. Some key people had been involved before, he says, and substance abuse was tolerated. Now he says, "If you're caught, you're terminated."

The third and fourth results are related. "We now have a freedom to talk freely about God," Victor says, "and people are starting to listen." They call one man "The Preacher." A millwright who welds machinery and fixes chains and motors, he talks about God as he moves from one area of the mill to another. A father who is struggling with his teenager is opening up to The Preacher and has indicated that he wants to start going to church.

The last result is a new Victor. "God is working in my life," he told me, "and a lot of it is because of your praying. I can leave my Bible out at work and no one says anything about it. I look at it as I walk by, and it really helps me through my day. They used to call me 'the grumpy old man,' but now I say, 'Good morning' and have a happy smile instead of a frown." And it's not just an act; Victor has a passion that everyone he touches should know about God and his saving grace through Christ. In fact, I think someone could also call Victor "The Preacher."

The Writer

I have a slew of photos on my desk doors from my One Heart writer friends.

By the fall I started prayerwalking, just about everything good had fallen away from my friend Marlo. After years of infertility she had become pregnant only to lose the baby several months into the pregnancy. She also lost another baby of sorts when the publication of her novel was canceled midstream. Two lifelong dreams died within weeks of each other.

It was the next year, however, that she described as the hardest of her life. No baby. No book contract. "It seemed as though God had turned his back on me. It seemed as though he no longer loved me because the 'nothing' was worse than the 'losing,'" Marlo wrote in one of her e-mail messages. Discouragement weighed so heavily on her that she felt as though nothing good would ever happen to her again.

What kept Marlo going, she said, were the prayers of her friends. As I prayed for Marlo, I particularly asked for a release from the sense of abandonment by God she felt. That was the first prayer answered. The second answer was Bethany Ann—not my Bethany Anne, but her own baby girl, born a month ago as I write this. "Bethany" means "house of poverty," and Marlo chose this name purposefully. She said that once she experienced the loss of most of what was dear to her, she began to realize how great God was. "I had to release my hopes and dreams and finally and fully give myself into the hands of the Father—to let go and accept his peace, even if he never gave me what I so much desired. Only then were the prayers answered."

Ah, yes, they were. Shortly after Bethany Ann's conception, Marlo's book, *Cry Freedom,* began its rebirth—a third prayer answered. A happy P.S. is that three more books are on their way as well—one on infertility that will birth hopes in the lives of men and women who have also felt the "nothing" in their lives.

The Freshmen

Another photo is of my school, where "my kids" yearly become another branch of my family tree. Most of the students in my high school don't know that I pray for them. As I mentioned earlier, every Monday morning I walk around all three schools in town and pray for the administrators and teachers by name, as well as the school board members and students in my classes.

As I walk, I am visually reminded of prayer needs: the boys who hackey-sack behind the school; the students who feed the sheep, pigs, donkeys, and chickens each day; the baseball players who might not finish out the season because of their bad grades.

On that first Monday I began this prayerwalk, I had no idea what lay ahead. That evening the father of Paul, one of my students, would kill himself. After an hour of sobbing and a sleepless night, I was torn about what to do as Paul's teacher. We had just finished studying *Romeo and Juliet,* and I had planned to have the students write about the pair's alternatives to suicide. We had discussed at length the folly of the fictional characters' impulsiveness, and my students knew they would be writing on this subject in class the next day.

My heart was torn. I knew I couldn't go on as planned, but I also felt it important to minister to the kids' needs and to answer their questions. I still wanted them to recognize signs of suicide in a friend and to know what to do if depressed themselves. The next morning I still was uncertain what to do, so I devoted the whole time I was prayerwalking to praying for the grieving family and for my students. As I was on my last lap toward home, I spotted walking sisters Jan and Lori and merged into their path. I saw on their faces the same ache that must have been on mine, and I told them of my quandary.

Lori, who works for the county social services department, immediately told me to call Anne, a county social worker. "She'll come, and she'll know what to do," Lori said.

I knew that God had brought Lori into my path that morning, so I called Anne. She and a coworker drove an hour to my school and answered questions for my freshmen classes that afternoon. I knew God's hand was in it all because they even suggested that students seek out their own pastors' counsel. And both women met afterward privately with thirteen students, a mix of boys and girls— two of whom had threatened suicide that school year, plus another who had witnessed her best friend's suicide three years earlier.

I often feel as though God literally brings answers into my pathway as I prayerwalk. That certainly was the case with Lori that day. If I hadn't met up with her and her sister that morning, I don't know what I would have done for my students. As it was, they received answers, counseling, comfort, understanding, and information about how they could also offer comfort. I felt the healing hand of God in my classroom.

The Skateboard Lady

I don't know if Diane knew I prayed for her, at least in the beginning. Diane and her husband, Jim, owned a video rental business in our downtown, just one shop off the beaten Main Street track. As I have prayed for all the business owners, I had prayed for Diane. I prayed that she would come to a deep faith in Christ, that her business would prosper, and that through these graces she would glorify God.

I loved the extra touches in Diane's shop, which was remade from a little rental cottage. In two back rooms homemade and other gift items were displayed, and next to the video counter sat a wealth of gear for skateboarders—shirts, board decals, and other items, many of them reading "Skateboarding Is Not a Crime." Diane served on a committee—a few adults and lots of kids—that advocated a local skate park. Although there are lots of organized sports activities offered through the schools, some kids' sport is skateboarding. And it's hard to work out your jumps and tricks in a town that has outlawed skateboarding on public property. Consequently, this slightly graying, hip sixty-year-old grandma was working with local kids to seek grant money and other funds to build a skate park.

I was surprised when I first saw Diane come to church about a year ago. I didn't know that was a first step toward a prayer answer, as Diane was then beginning her search to know God personally. We often start that search with a need, and hers was to quit smoking. She joined a small group that meets on Thursday nights and there found support, good teaching, and loving friendship.

The Sunday she invited Christ into her life she was afraid she would disappoint our pastor, David. He was on vacation that weekend and would miss the joy of hearing her profession of faith. A lay minister, Bill, was preaching that Sunday and made the invitation from Revelation 3:20: "Here I am! I stand at the door and knock. If anyone hears my voice and opens the door, I will come in and eat with him, and he with me." She opened the door that Sunday, and God took residence in her soul.

Two dichotomous changes occurred in her life. She began to live, and she began to die. Although she conquered smoking, smoking conquered her: Lung cancer quickly spread throughout her body. But a new hope and inner vitality took over as Diane's disease advanced. During the few short weeks she was ill, Diane testified greatly to God's goodness in her life. She told the church congregation one morning that she had hope—that whatever happened in her life, God was good.

There are some days when I wonder if my prayerwalking utterances do any good. I try to show concrete examples of my caring as well. Diane's health continued to decline, so I took a corned-beef dinner to her home one night. I met her daughter at the door.

"How's Diane?" I asked as I set the hot dishes on the counter.

The daughter gestured, and I watched as the formerly spunky, skateboard-advocating Diane shuffled across the adjoining room, tethered by her oxygen hookup.

"She can't come to the door," her daughter apologized.

"It's okay," I said, adding a little too weakly, "Hi, Diane."

She had asked for baptism. In our church we "save them up" for Easter Sunday. But as she quickly became confined to a hospital bed in her home, and as it became apparent that she wouldn't make it another month to Easter, a sprinkling was set for the next Sunday in her home. She didn't even make it to Sunday.

But Diane received a baptism of grace. She was in great pain the Thursday night before her scheduled baptism, and as Pastor David was visiting with her, he prayed for comfort and strength. He reported that God sprinkled grace over her, and she sighed with relief. Diane died the next morning.

How were prayers answered? Diane *did* come to a deep faith in Christ. Her life *did* glorify God, even as she died. And because she was an advocate for kids, I feel certain that the business she and her husband, Jim, owned mattered in our small town. And by the way, she didn't want flowers at her funeral that Saturday. Just a contribution to S.K.A.T.E. Her death may help to bring about a dream for kids in our town. And I think God will smile down on those skaters when they do their 360-degree flips.

A Daddy and a Daughter

My dad's picture sits at eye level to my right. In good health when the photo was taken a couple years ago, he sports a full smile almost as wide as his light gray Stetson. His light-sensitive glasses tinted orange don't match his pink complexion and hide his clear blue eyes, while his black sports coat blends in with the dark background. And someone who didn't know him well would have to look closely to notice that his apparently conservative tie is actually a Mickey Mouse design.

When I began prayerwalking, my dad was experiencing some crazy physical symptoms. They had accelerated about three months before, when Dad and Mom motored to our mountain home at five thousand feet elevation for Justin's high school graduation. It was a real kick watching Justin climb to the platform to accept ten scholarships and two prestigious awards, but I became concerned when Dad couldn't even climb the six steps to our house afterward without collapsing from exhaustion.

That trip to our home, just three hours away from theirs, would be Dad's last. Later that summer he started carting around an oxygen tank. Soon Mom was outdriving him in golf. And when he began losing muscle control in his left arm, Mom did all the driving.

Then one day, after endless examinations, MRIs, pulmonary tests, blood work, and a bone scan, we five kids each got the October phone call we'll never forget.

"I'm afraid I have to tell you," Mom said, "that your father has Lou Gehrig's disease."

Silence.

"Do you know what that means?" she added.

I did. I would later read everything I could find on amyotrophic lateral sclerosis (ALS), the disease that claimed the life of one of baseball's best—even his name. But at that moment on the phone with my mom, I already knew that Dad was suffering from a disease that would eventually take away all his muscle control—even swallowing and breathing. I knew it was an ugly, horrible way to leave the world. And I knew that my dear father, who had managed large department stores and hundreds of people in his lifetime, would soon not even be able to manage his own simplest functions.

The holidays were bittersweet. That Thanksgiving our family stood, thirty-some strong, hand-in-hand around the dining room table, and listened while Dad said grace. His speech was already beginning to slur, but everyone could hear "Thank you, Lord, for this wonderful family" tacked on to the traditional "Bless, O Lord, these gifts to our use and us to thy service…"

As usual, he stopped before the "amen," waiting for anyone to offer up a special thanks, but it was fairly silent that year. We were all too choked up at the thought it could be Dad's last Thanksgiving at the table. The emotional moment soon gave way to family chatter, but I watched as my outgoing sister-in-law Joyce cut my dad's meat and teased him about eating all his food. He was rapidly losing weight because it was getting harder for him to swallow.

When I visit my folks, I prayerwalk their neighborhood, which is in an outlying area of Sacramento. I don't walk in the dark since there are loads of skunks—some literal, some figurative—but the daylight walking is pleasant, and I usually focus on the prayer needs of my extended family while I'm there. That fall Dad and Mom always headed my prayer list. We remained aggressively positive and hopeful because we had read that the after-diagnosis life span was two to four years and that breakthroughs were being made in ALS and other muscular-dystrophy-related diseases. The threat of long-term bed care seemed ominous, however, and I prayed God would be merciful.

At Christmas I watched as Dad received what would be his last "haircut" from my daughter—not my older one, my younger one. It was a service Bethany, then six, performed only for her grand-father. As Dad would sit in his wooden Windsor chair and watch television in the family room, Bethany would gather her tools—brush, comb, shampoo, and scissors. Unlike most scissors, these were easy to locate, as they were actually her fingers. She'd then give Grandpa's silvery wisps the works—massage, imaginary shampoo, cut, and style. Now, I've sat in our local barbershop with my sons over the years and know that a good cut takes only about fifteen to twenty minutes. But Bethany was much more meticulous; hers could take an hour or more. For her good and faithful service Dad would compensate her richly with the contents of his change pocket.

Dad would always ask, "How much do I owe you?"

Bethany would answer, "Whatever you want, Grandpa."

And he'd answer, "Oh, I don't have that much."

He would have given each of us the world if he could have.

I didn't understand why my prayers weren't working. A month later Dad and Mom sought help at a special ALS clinic, and he started a drug that should have slowed the disease's progression. By my visit that month he was relying on a walker's help when he escorted my sister and me to the side fence to view the new baby calf next door. By the next month he could barely make it to the kitchen table and needed Mom's help feeding him Chinese takeout.

But still I clung to the doctor's and others' prognoses of two to four years of life.

Dad fell and went to the hospital a couple times the next month, but I felt okay about taking my gifted students to the Oregon Shakespeare Festival. He was eating better and even cracking jokes with the nurses. He couldn't manipulate the remote control very well and asked for a different remote that could move his bed and change television channels more easily.

The nurse got him one and said, "Now I want you to call me if you need anything at all."

"Okay," Dad said, "but what should I call you?"

Later that day he asked my mom tenderly, "Is this you and me?"

My prayers were answered the next day. When I returned from Oregon late that night and got the call that Dad probably wouldn't make it through the night, I drove the three-hour trip in record time. I prayed the whole way that God would be merciful, that he would allow me to see Dad before he passed away. But I didn't make it in time. And frankly, I felt cheated. I had faithfully prayed for healing for my dad. I had petitioned the Creator to help researchers find a cure for this horrible disease that had taken my father in less than five months. I had passionately prayed that I would at least be able to say good-bye. None of that happened. And the last request seemed so little. Just a good-bye? Why couldn't God have given me that?

One morning on a prayerwalk close to the one-year anniversary of Dad's death, I was still wrestling with this hurt as I watched a sunrise blossom above Elephant Head. Soft layers of cirrus clouds hovered like music staff lines above the elephant's back. Under each layer a yellow glow was turning gradually into a soft peach hue. I've seen a lot of sunrises on early morning walks but never one that lasted the whole hour.

The lasting beauty of that morning impressed upon my heart simply that *God is good.* My merciful God was good and had answered my prayers for my dad. He allowed Dad to slip into his heavenly arms—into beauty and away from pain—and spared Dad from a vegetative lifestyle. Dad was so adamant that he not lay uselessly in a bed, unable even to tell a joke. So God was good. And my prayer was answered: No. And the *No* was God's good way of honoring my dad. My request that Dad hang on was selfish. *No* was the right answer to my prayers.

If I hadn't prayerwalked and seen the infinite beauty and goodness in that sunrise, how long would I have waited in continued anger and brewing bitterness? I don't know. Maybe a day, maybe a week, maybe a lifetime.

All I know is this: Answers to my prayers come when I prayerwalk. The more I seek out God each morning, the more I am seeing him throughout the rest of my day and in the folks who appear in the photos on my desk doors and along the streets of my town.

I pray you'll meet him in your town as well.

Your Personal Trainer is waiting on the steps of your home. You don't need anything fancy to start; your open eyes and willing heart are the only crucial pieces of equipment he will need. Immediately he will lead you down an exciting path that will transform you into a woman of prayer, strength, and discipline.

I'll be praying for you!

A Letter to the PrayerWalk Study Guide Leader

Dear friend,

If you thumb the pages of this study guide, you'll notice that each chapter's questions are divided into the following three sections:

Warm up! These questions are designed as ice breakers—to get women talking and relating with one another and to anticipate the content of the chapter. If your group normally lasts an hour, you'll want to spend no more than ten to fifteen minutes on this section.

PrayerWalk...into the Word. These questions will direct you to scriptures that have been cited in the chapter and will introduce new scriptures. They will be analytical and interpretive in nature, helping each woman think about what the passage means to her. In an hour-long class, you'll probably devote a half-hour to this part of the study.

S-t-r-e-t-c-h out! Leave the last fifteen to twenty minutes of your hour for these closing questions. They will challenge the women in your group to think about how to apply the ideas from the chapter to their own lives.

Thank you so much for digging into *PrayerWalk*. I pray that your study of this book will dramatically change your life and the lives of the women in your study.

Blessings!

Janet

Chapter 1: If I Can Do It, You Can Do It

Warm Up!

1. What do you think of when you hear the words *discipline* or *self-control?*
2. Do you view yourself as disciplined? If not, would you like to be called disciplined? Why or why not?
3. If there were a Ms. Discipline, what do you think she'd look like? How would she spend a typical weekday, hour by hour?

Prayer Walk...into the Word

4. Read Proverbs 31:10-31. What words would you use to describe this woman?
5. How does this woman compare with your definition of Ms. Discipline?
6. In what ways are you similar to the Proverbs 31 woman? How are you different?

S-t-r-e-t-c-h Out!

7. How would you describe yourself physically? Emotionally? Spiritually?
8. What changes in lifestyle do you think God would have you make so that you are in a healthier condition?
9. Do you currently have a daily prayer time? If so, describe it.
10. How would you like your prayer life to change?

Chapter 2: Spiritual Endorphins

Warm Up!

1. When have been the happiest moments of your life?
2. How would you define *joy?*
3. When do you experience joy in your everyday life?
4. What is the difference, if any, between those happy times and the joy-filled ones?

Prayer Walk...into the Word

5. What are the people in the following passages doing that brings joy?
   - Leviticus 9:24
   - Deuteronomy 16:13-15
   - 2 Chronicles 30:1-26
6. Read James 1:2-3. When else are we to experience joy?
7. What are similar characteristics of joy between the James passage and those listed earlier?

S-t-r-e-t-c-h Out!

8. When are those times when you feel closest to God? Are those the times of joy? Why or why not?
9. What hindrances to joy do you find in your life?
10. How could a regular prayer routine maintain the joy in your life?

Chapter 3: Making Time

Warm Up!

1. How do you go about making decisions? Are you a Decider or a Feeler? Do you decide quickly or do you deliberate about something for a long time? Why, do you think?

Prayer Walk...into the Word

2. Read 2 Corinthians 4:16-18. What do you think it means when it says to fix your eyes on the unseen?
3. How could it be possible to have a godly focus all during your day?
4. Read Luke 10:38-42, and rephrase the story in your own words.
5. How did Jesus respond to Martha?
6. What kind of a hostess are you—a Martha or a Mary?
7. Would that change if Jesus knocked on your front door one day?

S-t-r-e-t-c-h Out!

8. Make a list of the ten people or activities that are the most important to you. Then write down what your usual Monday through Friday schedule is. Categorize what you did (for instance, work, housework, hygiene, fixing meals, eating meals, kids' games, family time, Bible study, and prayer), and add up the hours in each category. Compare the two lists.

9. What times during the day are the least productive or least satisfactory to you? How could you reorder your day to meet regularly in prayer and Bible study with God?
10. What changes in your life would this require?

Chapter 4: Why Walk?

Warm Up!
1. How do you view yourself—the way you look, the way you are?
2. How do you think God views you?

Prayer Walk...into the Word
3. Read Psalm 139:13-16 aloud. List everything in those verses that states something about who you really are.
4. Read Proverbs 3:1-8. How could the daily practice of prayer be a way to pursue godly wisdom and as a side benefit, "health to your body"?
5. List the promises in these verses, as well as your obligations in pursuit of these promises.

S-t-r-e-t-c-h Out!
6. Are you at risk for any disease or other physical problem? Which one(s)?
7. What are you currently doing for exercise?
8. How might walking help you develop a healthier lifestyle?
9. How might you benefit by combining the disciplines of walking and praying?

10. If prayerwalking is beginning to make sense to you, make a plan using the following guide and pray about it.
    • When could you prayerwalk?
    • Where is the best route?
    • How far will you go the first time?
    • What will be your eventual distance goal?
    • In what time frame would you reach these goals?
    Note: Before you actually start walking, you should review the suggestions in chapter 5.

Chapter 5: Reducing Aches and Pains

Warm Up!

1. What experiences do you have with walking as an exercise?
2. Have you encountered any physical problems in the past with any exercise routine you have started?
3. What "rules" for walking were suggested in chapter 5? Were any of these a surprise for you?

PrayerWalk...into the Word

4. Read 1 Corinthians 6:19-20, and explain why it's good to take care of your body. What could your physical shape have to do with your spiritual example?
5. Who, according to Deuteronomy 3:18, were chosen for a challenging physical assignment? Is there anything you feel you're missing out on with your current physical condition?

6. How are prayer and strength connected in Nehemiah 6:9?

7. Read 1 Corinthians 9:24-27. What prize do you think Paul had in mind when he wrote this? What prize or prizes might you have in mind as you begin prayerwalking?

8. Read Mark 9:43-48. How might it be possible to focus more on your body, the walking, and the physical benefits than on prayer? How will you stay focused on prayer?

S-t-r-e-t-c-h Out!

9. List any goals you have for improvement of your physical condition and pray about these. Do you feel God would agree?

10. Make another list of anything you might need before you begin your first prayerwalk. Then get ready, get set...go!

Chapter 6: PrayerWalk Partners

Warm Up!

1. Have you ever felt isolated or lonely? If so, when and what were the circumstances?

2. Have you ever had a prayer partner or an exercise partner? If so, what benefits did you find from that relationship?

PrayerWalk...into the Word

3. Read Philippians 2:4. How could prayerwalking with someone be a help to that other person?

4. In what areas of your life could a prayerwalking partner help you be more accountable?

5. Read Hebrews 10:25. What encouragement could you and a prayerwalking partner bring to each other?

6. Read Matthew 7:7-8. Sometimes we forget to pray for ourselves. How could a partner's prayers in your behalf be helpful?

7. What situations in your life do you feel could benefit from the support of others' prayers?

8. Read Matthew 18:19-20. How might prayerwalk partnering increase the effectiveness of your prayers?

S-t-r-e-t-c-h Out!

9. There may be one or more women who also need the prayer strength a partner could bring. Think of the many relationships in your life. Who might be a likely candidate as your prayerwalking partner one or more times a week?

10. After you have prayed about this, when might be a good time to suggest this to your friend?

Chapter 7: Prayer Tips from My Personal Trainer

Warm Up!

1. Who is a model for you as a pray-er?

2. What is it about that person that inspires you?

PrayerWalk...into the Word

3. *Jesus' intercession.* Read the Lord's Prayer in either Matthew 6:9-13 or Luke 11:2-4. How would you outline that prayer?

4. *Jesus' praise.* Read Matthew 11:25-26 and John 12:27-28. For what does Jesus praise God? Think of how God has taught you recently. For what could you also praise him?

5. *Jesus' thanksgiving.* Read John 11:41 and list several recently answered prayers for which you could thank God.

6. *Jesus' passion.* Sometimes we just need to spill our heart in prayer. Read John 17:1-26. Summarize what Jesus prays in this prayer after the Last Supper. What would you like to spill out to God in prayer?

7. Read the two Garden of Gethsemane prayers in Matthew 26:39 (or Mark 14:36 or Luke 22:42) and Matthew 26:42. What can we ask in prayer? What should we be willing to give up in prayer?

8. We know of three of Jesus' prayers on the cross. Read them in Luke 23:34, Matthew 27:46 (or Mark 15:34), and Luke 23:46. What changes of mood or feeling does Jesus express?

S-t-r-e-t-c-h Out!

9. Who needs your forgiveness today? Pray about calling that person soon.

10. Have you ever felt forsaken by God? If so, when? If you feel that way now, read Matthew 28:20 and write out that verse as a promise that he is near.

Chapter 8: "Great Is Thy Faithfulness"

Warm Up!

1. Recall a recent time when someone thanked you. How did you feel?

2. Now remember the last time you thanked someone else in person. What was your motivation behind that thank-you, and how do you think that person felt?

Prayer Walk...into the Word

3. Read 1 Chronicles 16:8-36. How many different ways could your praise be formed according to the Chronicles verses?

4. What are all the reasons you could list for praising God?

5. Paul often began his letters by remarking, as he did in Philippians 1:3, that he continually thanked God for his churches. Think through your regular daily schedule and the rooms and places you go. List as many things, circumstances, or people as you can who are reasons for thanking God.

6. Read Habakkuk 2:20 and Zechariah 2:13. How can silence be a form of awestruck prayer? Spend a few minutes in silent prayer, focusing on the goodness of God.

S-t-r-e-t-c-h Out!

7. For what characteristics of God (such as faithfulness, patience, and justice) are you especially appreciative today? Get up out of your chair and go outside or look out a window. Find as many additional reasons in your surroundings for praising God.

8. Write a poem or sing a song of praise to God. It doesn't have to rhyme!

9. Write a thank-you note to God for something he has recently done for you.

10. Is there someone God has recently used in your life who has encouraged you? Write that person a real note today and mail it. Remember to thank God, too!

Chapter 9: Take a Walk with Me

Warm Up!

1. What prayer concerns weigh most heavily upon you right now?

Prayer Walk...into the Word

2. Read Matthew 14 and make a list of all the reasons for prayer Jesus encountered on what appears to be one day of his life.

3. How do you think he spoke to his Father about these people or situations?

4. Look up the three recorded times we have of the Father speaking to or about Jesus: Matthew 3:17 (also Mark 1:11 and Luke 3:22), Matthew 17:5 (also Mark 9:7 and Luke 9:35), and John 12:28. What is the gist of these words?

S-t-r-e-t-c-h Out!

5. Think about a route you are considering for prayerwalking or one you have already started in your prayerwalk. List as many

businesses or people's homes as you can remember that lie along that route.

6. What people might you pass who would be either walking or driving?

7. If you took a different route, how might your prayers change?

8. List some prayer needs that arise out of your church family.

9. What law-enforcement or government employees might need your prayers?

10. Are there members of your extended family who have prayer needs? Which ones? Can you think of someone in your life for whom no one else might remember to pray? Pray now for all those folks.

Chapter 10: Eyes Wide Open

Warm Up!

1. What struggles with sin do you regularly face?

Prayer Walk...into the Word

2. Read Luke 10:1-24. How did the seventy-two believers respond after their travels, and why?

3. According to verses 18-24, how did Jesus respond to their news?

4. Read 2 Corinthians 10:1-6, and explain what authority a believer has according to this passage.

5. In Ephesians 6:10-18 Paul lists how a believer should prepare herself for spiritual warfare. List all the ways he suggests that we get ready for these battles.

6. In practical ways, how could we do those things? What weapon is the weakest in your life, and how could you "practice" with it more?

S-t-r-e-t-c-h Out!

7. How might you pray for God's help in overcoming your personal struggles?
8. What widespread weaknesses have you observed in your community?
9. What ones particularly weigh upon your heart and why?
10. Read Romans 12:21, and pray now for God to overcome this evil with his good.

Chapter 11: A Sacrifice of Tears

Warm Up!

1. Have you wanted something in prayer so badly that you felt your tears were prayers? If so, what were the circumstances of those prayers?
2. What were the answers to your prayers? Or are you still praying?

PrayerWalk...into the Word

3. *Tears of intercession.* When have you felt like David in Psalm 39:12?
4. *Tears of remorse.* Why are the women weeping in Luke 23:26-31? How does Jesus suggest that they redirect their tears?

5. What circumstances in your past do you regret? If you have not repented, say or write out that prayer now. Then read 1 John 1:9 and accept God's forgiveness.

6. *Tears of joy.* Read Psalm 126. Often we sow burdens on our prayerwalks—entrusting them to God's care—and later he turns them into a joy-filled harvest. How has a former burden become a source of joy in your life?

7. *Tears of suffering with God.* Read Isaiah 44:6-23. What sin does man commit?

8. How does God feel, do you think? How does God respond?

9. How do you feel about man's sin and God's response?

S-t-r-e-t-c-h Out!

10. How would you like to "grow up" in prayer?

Chapter 12: Faces of Answered Prayer

Warm Up!

1. What answered prayers have most encouraged you in your life? Why?

PrayerWalk...into the Word

2. In Genesis 24:12-18 how is Abraham's servant's prayer answered before he even finishes it? Have you ever learned that you had a prayer answered before you had prayed it?

3. How does God answer the Israelites' grumbling prayers in Exodus 16:3-4? Describe a time when you thought God

had forgotten about your prayers and then later you learned otherwise.

4. How does God answer Gideon's prayers in Judges 6:36-40? When did God confirm some important decision for you with a sign?

5. Read Psalm 18:1-3. Like David, have you clearly been saved by God from a difficult situation?

6. Why does God give Solomon more than he asked in 1 Kings 3:5-14? When have you received more than you asked for from God?

7. What risk does Elijah take in 1 Kings 18:20-39? How does he pray? When have you prayed a bold prayer, and what was its result?

8. Why will King Josiah not have to witness disaster during his lifetime, according to 2 Chronicles 34:26-28? For whom are you praying to turn to God in faith?

S-t-r-e-t-c-h Out!

9. Have you begun prayerwalking yet? If you have, what answers to prayer have you already experienced? If you haven't begun yet, when will you start?

10. What "impossible" situations could you give over to prayer in your next prayerwalk?

Resources on Walking

Fitness Walking for Dummies by Liz Neporent (Foster City, Calif.: IDG Books, 2000). This is the thickest of the volumes and, like other Dummies books, covers everything possible in a readable fashion. The author has written several fitness books and has a master's degree in exercise physiology.

I liked the feature called "Jargon Alert," which defines buzz-words.

I didn't like the cost. It's the priciest—mine cost $20—but it's a complete resource.

Fitness Walking for Women by Anne Kashiwa and James Rippe, M.D. (New York: Perigee, 1987). An aerobic instructor and cardiologist succinctly provide the basics on walking, with lots of charts and pictures. This is a good resource for stretching exercises.

I liked the focus on women's concerns. There's a great chapter for the pregnant walker.

I didn't like the chapter on adventure walking because it won't reach the average woman.

The 90-Day Fitness Walking Program by Seth Bauer and Mark Fenton (New York: Perigree, 1995). These *Walking* magazine editors lay out a daily, two-page reading and challenge on walking. A small chart provides spaces to write daily walking achievements.

I liked the focus on encouragement.

I didn't like that some essential information is not presented until the end of the book. Read it through, then reread it during your ninety-day plan.

Prevention's Practical Encyclopedia of Walking for Health: From Age Reversal to Weight Loss, the Most Complete Guide Ever Written by Mark Bricklin and Maggie Spilner (Emmaus, Penn.: Rodale Press, 1992). These *Prevention* magazine editors compiled monthly articles on walking and created an A to Z guide on walking issues, from dogs to mall walking to vacations. At the back of the book is a guide for a yearlong walking program, with weekly goals.

I liked the section on weights.

I didn't like some Eastern thought scattered throughout, including "The Zen Perspective."

Walking: A Complete Guide to the Complete Exercise by Casey Meyers (New York: Random House, 1992). This fitness writer is also a consultant for a walking shoe company. He provides a detailed, scientific examination of walking.

I liked its complete discussion of form.

I didn't like the scientific jargon and references to evolution.

Walking: The Magazine of Smart Health and Fitness (Boston: A Reader's Digest Publication). Articles run the gamut; subjects range from personality to walking techniques and challenges to weight issues.

I like the annual March issue, which has the "Shoe Review."

I dislike some of the advertisements, including some for diet aids and sex-improvement videos.

Notes

Chapter Two: Spiritual Endorphins

1. See Psalm 46:1; Lamentations 3:23-24; John 15:19.

Chapter Three: Making Time

1. Oswald Chambers, *My Utmost for His Highest* (Uhrichsville, Ohio: Barbour, 1963), 180.

2. Dutch Sheets, *The River of God* (Ventura, Calif.: Gospel Light, 1998), 195, quoted in Joanna Weaver, *Having a Mary Heart in a Martha World* (Colorado Springs, Colo.: WaterBrook, 2000), 18.

3. John Stark, "Red Alert: Fiery Jamie Luner's Got Her Life in Motion," *Walking,* June 2000, 70-2.

Chapter Four: Why Walk?

1. Centers for Disease Control and Prevention, "Physical Activity and Health: A Report of the Surgeon General," http://www.cdc.gov (30 October 1999).

2. JoAnn Manson, et al., "A Prospective Study of Walking as Compared with Vigorous Exercise in the Prevention of Coronary Heart Disease," *New England Journal of Medicine* 341 (26 August 1999): 850-6.

3. American Heart Association, "Exercise (Physical Activity)," http://www.justmove.org (30 October 1999).

4. American Medical Association, "Brisk Daily Walking Markedly Reduces Risk of Type 2 Diabetes in Women," http://www.ama-assn.org (20 October 1999).

5. American Medical Association, "Daily Exercise Cuts Breast Cancer Risk by Up to 20% in Middle-Aged Women," http://www.ama-assn.org (27 October 1999).

6. President's Council on Physical Fitness, "Walking for Exercise and Pleasure," http://www.minorities-jb.com/foryour walkingf.html (27 October 1999).

7. President's Council on Physical Fitness, *Walking for Exercise and Pleasure.*

8. American College of Sports Medicine, "Does Exercise Help or Harm a Cold?" www.acsm.org (30 October 1999).

9. March of Dimes Birth Defects Foundation, "Fitness for Two," www.modimes.org (30 October 1999).

10. March of Dimes Birth Defects Foundation, "Fitness for Two."

11. American Association of Retired Persons, "Pep Up Your Life with Exercise," www.aarp.org (30 October 1999).

12. American Association of Retired Persons, "Pep Up Your Life with Exercise."

Chapter Five: Reducing Aches and Pains

1. Liz Neporent, *Fitness Walking for Dummies* (Foster City, Calif.: IDG Books, 2000), 97-146.

2. Casey Meyers, *Walking: A Complete Guide to the Complete Exercise* (New York: Random House, 1992), 72.

Chapter Seven: Prayer Tips from My Personal Trainer

1. The ten prayers are

   a. Lord's Prayer, Matthew 6:9-13 and Luke 11:2-4

   b. Galilean prayer, Matthew 11:25-26

   c. Prayer before Lazarus is brought back to life, John 11:41-42

   d. Prayer after Triumphal Entry into Jerusalem, John 12:27-28

   e. Upper Room prayer, John 17:1-25

   f. First Gethsemane prayer, Matthew 26:39; Mark 14:36; and Luke 22:42

   g. Second Gethsemane prayer, Matthew 26:42

   h. First prayer on the cross, Luke 23:34

   i. Second prayer on the cross, Matthew 27:46 and Mark 15:34

   j. Third prayer on the cross, Luke 23:46

2. Jan Karon's Mitford series includes: *A Light in the Window* (1996);

At Home in Mitford (1996); *These High, Green Hills* (1997); *Out to Canaan* (1998); and *A New Song* (1999) (New York: Penguin).

Chapter Eight: "Great Is Thy Faithfulness"

1. Thomas O. Chisholm, "Great Is Thy Faithfulness," *The Hymnal for Worship and Celebration* (Waco, Tex.: Word Music, 1986), 43.

2. Great resources for learning about God's character are a trio of books: *Names of God* by Nathan Stone (Chicago: Moody, 1944); *Names of Christ* by T. C. Horton and Charles E. Hurlburt (Chicago: Moody, 1994); and *Names of the Holy Spirit* by Ray Pritchard (Chicago: Moody, 1995).

3. C. S. Lewis, *Letters to Malcolm: Chiefly on Prayer* (New York: Harcourt, Brace, & World, 1964), 11.

4. Saint Augustine, *Confessions of a Sinner* (New York: Penguin, 1995), 2.

5. From "O, Come All Ye Faithful." Originally written as "Adeste Fideles" by John Francis Wade in 1744 and translated into English by Frederick Oakeley about one hundred years later. "Adeste Fideles" means "be present or near, ye faithful." (Kenneth Osbeck, *Joy to the World! The Stories Behind Your Favorite Christmas Carols* [Grand Rapids: Kregel, 1999], 49-50.)

Chapter Nine: Take a Walk with Me

1. Elfrida Jones Vipont, *A Book of Prayers for Children* (New York: Harcourt, 1948), 46.

2. Thomas Olden, *The Epistles and Hymn of Saint Patrick* (Dublin: Hodges, Foster & Co., 1876), 105-9. This section of verse comes from "The Breastplate," also titled "The Secundinus Hymn of St. Patrick," by Thomas Olden. It is believed that either a nephew or disciple of Saint Patrick wrote the hymn in the fifth century.

3. The Father's words to and about Jesus are recorded in Matthew 3:17, Mark 1:11, and Luke 3:22 (after his baptism by John); in Matthew 17:5, Mark 9:7, and Luke 9:35 (at the Transfiguration); and in John 12:28 (after the Triumphal Entry).

Chapter Ten: Eyes Wide Open

1. Richard Foster, *Prayer: Finding the Heart's True Home* (San Francisco: Harper, 1992), 229.

Chapter Eleven: A Sacrifice of Tears

1. *Webster's Seventh New Collegiate Dictionary*, s.v. "professional."

2. Henri J. M. Nouwen, *With Open Hands: Bring Prayer into Your Life* (New York: Ballantine, 1972).